Not a Stranger to Storms

TEMI FAGADE

Not a Stranger to Storms

TEMI FAGADE

Not a Stranger to Storms

Copyright © 2018 by Temi Fagade

Paperback ISBN 978-0-9862234-9-5

Published by
Dewalette Creations
dewalette@gmail.com

Printed in the United States of America

Dedication

I'm giving this to You, Precious Holy Spirit. I relish and celebrate diverse encounters with and in You. This Christian walk seems so easy as You show up time and time again thereby affirming my faith. Ah! What would I do without You, Sweet Holy Spirit? I truly celebrate and cherish Your presence within me.

Thank you for rebuke, corrections, timely guidance, inspirations, revelations, quickening, help and all You do for me.

Eu Te Agradeco, Espirito Santo De Deus!

Acknowledgments

I acknowledge the husband of my youth, Omotayo Fagade, thank you for believing in me and for making room for full expression of God`s mandate in my life, You remain a pillar any day. To our three covenant blessings: David, Deborah and Mateuzinho; quivers you three will always be. Thank you for the unwavering support and for believing in this project; indeed we make a team!

To my parents, Mr Theophilus & Mrs Adenike Ayeni thank you for the bond of family. To my three siblings Tolu, Tayo and Dayo, I can always depend on you as Aaron, Ur and Joshua to lift up my arms for victory till all Amalekites are completely smitten. To my second Daddy, Mr Adedamola Adams, thank you sir for painstakingly going through the manuscript; your ever encouraging words and prayer sure mean much. Your liberal soul be made fat sir

My indebtedness goes to many individuals in the faith and bodies of Christ who have at one time or the other contributed in no small measure to nurturing the Holy seed that was birthed in me at salvation.

I have been nourished, discipled and privileged to serve in many ministries as I relocated to various locations at different phases of my life. Worthy of mention are the Student Christian Movement University of Ibadan, Glory Tabernacle Ministries Ibadan, The Redeemed Christian Church of God, Okota –Lagos and Aberdeen Scotland, World Alive Ministries, Port Harcourt, The Men of Issachar Vision, Brazil and the Winners Chapel, Worldwide.

I cannot but give special recognition to a Father of Fathers, one whom the Lord has used to ignite the faith fire in me in the person of Bishop David Olaniyi Oyedepo. Respect Papa! Thank you for obeying the Liberation Mandate.

On this book project, your support has been overwhelming Isekhua Evborokhai and Olukemi Oluwole, truly, helpers of destiny you two are! And of a truth, your helpers shall not be few. Thank You!

Continually, I pledge my allegiance to the lamb.

Contents

◢

Contents

Foreword

༄

The Storms of Life are things we cannot escape from as long as we sojourn here on earth. Storms come to everyone in their own season. However, we must take cognizance of the fact that the presence of storms does not mean the absence of God. God never promised a storm-free life but one of the attributes of storms is that it makes a tree to take deeper roots. Our faith grows deeper after each storm, thus making us victorious in Christ.

In a contemporary rendition of the story told by Jesus in Matthew 7:24 and Luke 6:47-49, both men went to the same church, because they both "heard these words of mine". Both had the privilege of listening to the same divine truth. Both men were actually "bibliocentric" but they did not have the same conclusion. Any believer can read, hear, preach or teach God's Word, but only a true disciple of Christ will seek to excitedly do the words of Christ. It is the willingness, mind set or resolution to be doers of the word of Christ that distinguishes an ardent follower of Christ from a passive believer in Christ.

In other words, the primary reason why many believers today are only "excited hearers" but "reluctant doers" of God's word is our ability to mix the word with faith in our heart in forming a solid rock. Hebrews 4:2 says, *"For unto us was the gospel preached, as well as unto them: but the word preached did not profit them, not being mixed with faith in them that heard it."*

In the parable told by Jesus, the two men were subject to the same storm; the rain descended, the floods came, the winds blew and beat upon their houses. The result for the foolish builder was "it fell" but for the wise builder "it fell not". Jesus said if we follow Him, we would be like the wise builder. We will come through the inevitable storms of life, the trials and difficulties that accompany life. Rightly appropriating His word is good ground because His teachings are rock-solid principles on how to live as overcomers.

While crossing to the other side on a boat trip on the sea of Galilee, a storm arose that threatened with tossing winds and the possibility of their boat being flooded. As they cried to Him in Mark 4:38, Christ arose and calmed the winds and waves with His power, saying, "Peace, be still" (Mark 4:39). He turned to His Apostles and asked, "Where is your faith?" (Luke 8:25). Christ gently chastised them for being fearful and not remembering that He could calm the tossing seas during a storm. Faith in the Lord and confidence in His words are anchors in overcoming any storm.

Temi, in her usual open, inspiring and engaging writing style makes this book an enjoyable read. She has detailed her various experiences in this book to reveal the reality of storms in the life of a Christian. Peeling through the treasures in this book provides an excellent reminder for Christians to know that "one person's testimony should be another person's possibilities".

I therefore recommend these true life encounters in print to all who cherish the assurance of victory in Christ over every storm.

Dr Sola Oduwole
Pastor, RCCG SA Province 2
Cape Town, South Africa

Introduction

∽

THERE HAVE BEEN SEVERAL TIMES in my life that I have had to completely trust in God when all I had left was my faith in Him! I must confess those periods were tough on me; but it was then I learnt to walk closer with God and love him deeper.

In the next few pages of this book, I will be sharing some of those experiences with you. You may be able to identify with them or not, but without a doubt I know God will come through for you as He did countless times for me, if you hold on to your faith.

Let me start off by saying that every believer has a measure of faith. This faith is given at the point of salvation.

Romans12v3 says; *"....in accordance with the faith God has distributed to each of you."*

And just like the saints of old, we have all received "great and precious promises" which includes our faith as we see in 2Peter1v1-4; with emphasis on verse 1. *"To those who through the righteousness of our God and Saviour Jesus Christ have received a faith as precious as ours."*

I would like to therefore submit that faith is a necessity in accomplishing the will of God in all spheres of life.

Oftentimes, in dealing with the problem we face, it is not the level or amount of faith we have but in the application of faith! As a matter of fact, the "mustard seed" size of faith suffices. That was what Jesus implied in His response when His disciples asked Him to increase their faith! You see, God does not give great faith to one and little faith to another. Romans12v3 confirms that God has apportioned to each a degree of faith.

All we need for a godly life has been freely given; however, we need to "plug" into the power source for "activation".

Understanding the truth of God's words makes us walk in faith. A genuine believer will not go far in actualizing God's plan for his or her life without faith. Habakkuk2v4 says: *"but the righteous person shall live by his faith"*.

Faith is the currency used in heaven; hence proper understanding and maximization of this heavenly currency assures unlimited access is granted to the resources therein. While everything comes from God and nothing is on our account, the responsibility of growing that faith lies on the believer.

This book is an earnest attempt at arousing the faith of every redeemed child of God. It is a charge to enforce the word of God in confronting life's challenges during our Christian sojourn. *Not A Stranger To Storms,* in its simplicity, contains some of my testimonies and stories intended to stir and provoke you in strengthening your faith to receive your victory in Christ.

It is the desire of the Father to see every Kingdom Ambassador walk in faith today as the saints of old once did. And as Hebrews 12v2 says, we *"look unto Jesus the author and finisher of our faith"* in obtaining manifestation of such promises.

God has fulfilled His part; the onus therefore rests on us as believers to actualize the finished work in every aspect of our individual lives.

It is my uttermost prayer that inspiration for great faith will be birthed afresh in you as you peel through the pages of this book. He will yet use us and every part of our lives' events for His glory.

Shalom!

Chapter 1

~

My Salvation
May 13, 1993

A S I PEN DOWN THIS CHAPTER, the testimony of my salvation experience floods back afresh. It was the period of the Presidential election in Nigeria. The campaign and election was different; there was this buzz going around campuses that for the first time after a long time we were going to have a civilian president! More importantly, it would bring an end to the military regime that had lasted for many years. Many Nigerians were looking forward to this.

Campuses were busy with members of the student union campaigning for their favourites. This was also the period when universities experienced an increase in cult activities; so, there was the usual caution as the entire university community and the entire country got ready to go to the polls on the 12th of June.

It was in the middle of this chaos that I had an encounter that saw me accepting the Lord Jesus as my Lord and Saviour at the University of Ibadan on the 13th day of May 1993.

Contrary to the experience many others told about their salvation experience, I had "gradually warmed up" to the Gospel.

You see, my first invitation to attend a fellowship on campus was to the Student Christian Movement, at the University of Ibadan, to which I completely ignored; but the brother who invited me was patient and persistent. In hindsight, I will say he was strategic! Interestingly, he was the twin brother of the boyfriend I had back then on campus.

I admired his consistency at visiting me and his constant reminder that I owe him an attendance or visit at the fellowship.

"So, when are you honouring my invitation to attend our fellowship? Please try, I know you'll be blessed…"

Those were the kind of words I received often.

At other times, he would say things like:

"Are we going together today?" or "We have a special program tonight that I think will really bless you…"

He just refused to give up asking and inviting.

Only heaven can tell how much intercession would have gone into the consistent invitation for the rescue of my soul.

So, after much persistence and persuasion, I finally decided to honour the invitation for once. After all, the fellowship only lasted for two hours and there was much of dancing amongst fellow students on campus. Music and dance was a great attraction to me I must confess.

Recalling that while passing by the Chapel of Resurrection within the University campus on a few occasions, I had often heard upbeat and rhythmic songs and the jubilation that typified youthful fellowship.

"So, it wouldn't be that bad." I had thought within me.

Being armed with the fellowship days and time, I opted to attend the following Sunday.

On this fateful Sunday evening, this brother was already waiting for me an hour before fellowship at the porter's lodge of my hall of residence. Either because he thought I would change my mind about attending or because he felt it was a duty he owed me, I cannot tell. I was however impressed that he came to pick me up; so, we left for fellowship.

The meeting kicked off about fifteen minutes after we arrived. The atmosphere was just "charged", for lack of words to describe the ambience I felt within the chapel that evening. There was something magical about the environment. I could see orderliness and a sense of purpose at large; there were ushers at the entrance welcoming everyone with smiles.

As I watched many others arrive, I noticed the manner of greetings. They were so chaste, respectful, smiling and honouring one another. Their mode of dressing also caught my attention. I quickly noticed most of the brothers had funny looking trousers and that all the sisters had scarves, berets or some form of covering on their heads with very few exceptions like myself. Many settled in to offer personal prayers before the meeting commenced.

I wasn't disappointed with the music; because it so turned out that the praise and worship session was superb that day. Honestly, I thoroughly enjoyed the singing and more especially, dancing! I had a swell time and once we sat down, I slept for about three quarters of the rest of the meeting. Whether the ushers made any attempt at waking me or not, I cannot tell. All I remember was that I enjoyed myself during the dance session but had not the faintest clue of anything else thereafter.

I was invited again and again, and repeatedly, this slumber would take over once we sat down. And then came this fateful fellowship meeting, it was on a Sunday night fellowship; a minister called Pastor Tosin Jegede was invited to minister. His words must have gotten through to me as sleep evaded me this time around. Some of the points he made were that sin is a ravenous monster which gives temporary pleasure initially but eventually enslaves one before leading to destruction. The fact that it cannot be conquered by one's self will and the need for that divine power to help one live a life that truly pleases God were words that sunk right into me that fateful evening.

For once, I heard part of the message, got convicted and as he made the altar call, I knew I had to respond. However, I held back and refused to step forward as he invited.

You see, that fellowship was what we referred to as the "SU – Scripture Union type" where the ladies must cover their heads, were not allowed to wear trousers or use make-up, and so on. I found the mode of dressing a bit archaic, too simple and rather inconvenient. I just would never be ready to live that kind of constrained, boring and wretched life. I thought to myself.

Some sisters from the fellowship who lived in the same hostel block where I resided on sighting me twice at the fellowship paid visits to my room.

In my mind, I had confessed that I wouldn't be caught dead with their kind of dress mode. Such mode of dressing just wasn't me. However, something kept drawing me to attend that fellowship again and again.

During the night of May 13th, 1993, the Spirit of God visited me with such strong conviction. The voice in my heart had asked why I was resisting His move in my life and with great contrition in my heart, tears welled up from within and I cried out. It was like seeing in a vision what appeared to be the image of Jesus Christ with those holes that pierced the hands. I just couldn't struggle anymore as I saw it all differently for once and felt so wretched and unworthy.

With such feeling of guilt and unworthiness, I asked Jesus to forgive and wash me of all my sins and that I wanted Him as my Lord and Saviour. I shed tears all night but then His peace flooded my heart.

You see, mine wasn't just a case of confession and acceptance. I was remorseful and was truly sorrowful for many days as I realized I had lived in sin and just wasn't worthy of His mercy and love. I could tell thereafter that I was a changed person.

Hymns and many worship songs from then on began to make

meaning to me and the lyrics ushered emotions that brought tears regularly as I contemplated the works of my Redeemer for me.

In no distant time, people started noticing the change in me. Though we had never conversed, a lady and fellow student who stayed two rooms away from mine confronted me to ask what happened to me and if I was now born again as she noticed I had changed. She said I had a glow she couldn't explain.

She was glad when I boldly told her I had accepted Christ into my life. She loudly praised God because of me.

"Oh, you don't know how much I had prayed for you asking the Lord to give you an encounter personally" she said.

Before my salvation experience, the mindset I had was that this new life in Christ was for the poverty stricken. At least that was the picture the enemy painted in my heart. He had succeeded in blindfolding me with such misconception for very long. Little wonder Apostle Paul said, *"In whom the god of this world hath blinded the minds of them which believe not, lest the light of the glorious gospel of Christ, who is the image of God, should shine unto them"* 2 Corinthians 4:4 (KJV).

As my presence became stronger at the fellowship meetings, I started receiving visits from brethren especially sisters from my hall of residence. Three things I was quick to observe about these sisters was the joy that oozed from within them. What aura of peace they had! The love and hand of fellowship they extended to me as well as hope expressed in all their conversations couldn't go unnoticed. They were so positive! I couldn't resist that love for long. Indeed, love conquers all.

Let me also confess that as a young convert then, there were days I never wanted to receive these sisters' visitations. I had often hidden behind the door when I recognised their voices at the door. My room mates would then cover up for me that I was not around. Why I did that, I sincerely can't tell or remember. Maybe the flesh was still dominant over the Spirit.

I must at this point mention that some of those sisters too were not as friendly as they didn't approve of my mode of dressing.

A young Christian must always remember that God is much more interested in the heart than the outward appearance. The Holy Spirit specializes in transforming from the inward to the outward. As we walk with Him and yield to His voice, the Holy Spirit addresses and convicts us of any aspect or issue of our individual lives that needs correction. His personal dealings with me must never be a standard for judging anyone. It's all about His personal leading. Little wonder the scripture admonishes personal conviction (Romans14v5 says: *"each should be fully convinced in their own mind"*).

It must be understood that I came from a background where my father took so much interest in the affairs of his children including their physical appearance. Regularly, he would ask what our needs were (especially for school purposes). Our bank accounts were regularly credited for every need. I was not born with a silver spoon in my mouth and neither did I hold one in my hand but as a family, we had all our needs met and even certain wants were supplied too. As a family, we could pass for well above average in every sense.

All in a bid to avoid the normal temptation girls on campus were exposed to, my parents ensured all our needs were superseded. I remember clearly that he had taken us to tailors to make jeans of an assortment of colours during my school days.

I recall my father once asking jokingly, "So what are your needs for school before daddy goes ahead to do 'fine boy' with money?"

My father till date remains one who believes in being polished with great finesse while giving optimum attention to details. He still happens to be the best English teacher I ever had. Before sending any letter to him, you would want to make sure all your 'I's were well dotted and your 'T's crossed, else, be ready for an English lesson on your next visit home.

Ours was a nominal Christian family. We attended a Baptist church as a family, showed respect for others and that was it.

And so, coming from a nominal Christian background, I was now being seen as the strange one. Indeed, I became different, a change that wasn't totally welcomed but observed for events to unfold. On such matters, my father could best be described as a very liberal man. It was therefore not a surprise when on one of my birthdays I overheard my father telling my mom that he bought me a tie 'n' dye batik material to sew believing that was commensurate with my new way of life. My younger sister, on the other hand, whose birthday was a few days after mine, received a two-piece trouser and top made of fine jersey material.

However, my salvation experience was so real and one never to be forgotten in a hurry. My faith grew stronger and my walk with the Lord grew deeper daily. It was lonesome except when I was at school and enjoyed the fellowship of the brethren. I however learnt to depend on Him more and grew to believe Him for the impossible. God on His part was too faithful; He was involved in every affair of my life as I looked up to Him. I enjoyed sweet communion with the Holy Spirit. Cultivating the act of living in His presence and the consciousness of His person were keys to invoking deeper communion in my personal walk.

Amidst many early experiences, two that remain indelible in my heart and memory occurred shortly after I gave my life to Christ.

I had lost a precious umbrella of mine and as I prayed about it, the Lord was quick to reassure me it would be found and much later that night He revealed where it was to me in a vision. The next morning, I just needed to walk into the pantry shop in my hall of residence only to see my umbrella hung behind the counter as a lost and found item.

Another incident happened between a senior friend and I. The person in question had offended me. I was deeply wounded within me however, there was little I could do, so, in my mind, I became closed up towards him. For me the best thing to do was to avoid and ignore him as much as possible. If he were my mate, the silent treatment or malice would have been the best option. So, with that closed mindset, I went to bed.

As I woke up the next morning, even before I could go far in observing my quiet time, I heard 1Peter2v1-2 in my spirit, *"So put aside every trace of malice and all deceit and hypocrisy and envy and all slander and hateful speech; 2 like newborn babies [you should] long for the pure milk of the word, so that by it you may be nurtured and grow in respect to salvation [its ultimate fulfillment]"* *(AMP).*

The very first phrase as I opened that scripture popped out at me:

"So put aside every trace of malice…...".

I needed no soothsayer; neither did I need to continue reading. It was already very clear and I just knew what the Spirit of God was referring to. Immediately I repented and amended my ways towards the person in question. And what peace I received after that incident! These, amongst other incidents gave me so much confidence that He was interested in every minute detail of my life.

Concerning the children of Israel, the Lord went as far in the book of Leviticus to tell them what to eat, what to wear, what to think, how to act, where to go, how to behave and even as far as giving them laws of hygiene. God was interested in every aspect of their lives just as He is in ours today. I stand as a living proof that His principles have not changed. It all depends on how much room we give Him in our lives and how yielded we are to Him. It's all a matter of exchanging our self-will for His will. God is ready to go as far as we are interested in this Christian walk with Him.

As I became more committed, I joined the evangelism team of my fellowship and preaching became a regular part of my weekly routine. Though I had little knowledge of scriptures, I was armed with my personal encounter and that zeal was key to my evangelism efforts. So, I began to gather other souls for Him while still under the tutelage of many in my fellowship. In no time, thereafter, the bible study coordinator invited me to join the bible study teaching group. My involvement ensured that I was being rooted and accompanying fruits were obvious. My commitment greatly influenced my spiritual growth. I learnt the place of communion and that of service distinctively.

In no time at all, His leading became much more real such that often after evangelism, the Lord would speak to me about how to evangelize, areas I needed to work upon and things to emphasize.

I was privileged also, as the Lord by His Spirit started revealing things to me about my future.

Till date, that voice hasn't been scarce, just as it was well over 24 years ago.

Chapter 2

Appendicitis

S
OMETIME IN LATE 1994, UNIVERSITIES experienced one of the frequent disruptions in the Academic sessions. This one was a strike by lecturers over salary increase and conditions of service.

As usual, many students capitalized on the opportunity to be away from school but I stayed back on campus for many reasons; one of which was that I thought the strike would end shortly. And again, I saw it as an opportunity to catch up on many courses, attend fellowship and evangelize. After about three weeks, it became obvious however that an end to the strike was nowhere in sight as days turned into weeks. And so, I decided to go home and visit with my family in Lagos.

On arrival, my immediate junior sister was in pain. A visit to the clinic revealed she needed to undergo appendectomy the next day. She did and when she returned home, we all rallied round her and were all so supportive while she recuperated.

Surprisingly, my only brother followed suit days after and had to undergo the same minor surgery. In a short space of weeks, it was my other sister's turn.

We wondered if it had anything to do with our diet; but it wasn't our diet but an attack of the enemy.

One evening shortly after my three siblings had all recovered; I felt this sharp pain on the lower part of my belly and as if I heard a voice saying, "your turn". I rushed to the study; I recall those were days when the internet and computer use was still unpopular in Nigeria so, the encyclopaedia was the source of retrieving information. I read up on the symptoms I had and from all indications, the description was that of appendicitis. But I wasn't going to accept it! Unfortunately for that uninvited guest called appendicitis, my Pastor, Dr Uzor Obed of Glory Tabernacle Ministries some weeks prior to that incidence had fed us a 3-day teaching on faith—one which I had ravenously digested.

You see, a few months back; in February of 1994, I joined a ministry called Glory Tabernacle Ministries in Ibadan while I was still committed to my fellowship on campus with fellowship meetings on Thursday and Sunday evenings. I attended Glory Tabernacle Sunday mornings and for special meetings because of the urge I had to feed my Spirit and know God more by hearing His Word. This helped my faith to grow! Little wonder the scripture says faith cometh by hearing; it is those words that give understanding which fires up faith.

Consequently, faith comes from hearing the message, and the message is heard through the word about Christ (Romans 10v17).

So, after confirming the symptoms through the encyclopedia, I immediately rejected appendectomy and reminded God that His holy one must not see corruption, and that no cut would pass my body. Then I called up a friend and we agreed together in prayer.

However, the pain did not subside and though I wasn't walking straight up, I believed God would heal me.

As a believer, you must believe even in the presence of fear irrespective of what you see or feel. So, I had been taught to believe and confess the word. Faith can also be interpreted to mean 'believing that it is okay even when all is not okay'.

My mom noticed I was walking a bit bent and immediately called my father's attention. They chided me for my 'SU/fanatical beliefs' saying it was just a minor surgery that all my siblings had undergone and recovered quickly from.

A visit to the doctor revealed it was best I be operated the next morning. One thought that reverberated in my mind was the urgency for surgery for each member of the family. One minute, everyone was fine and then the next minute, the need for appendectomy.

As we retired to bed that night, I told God He had to show up on time and my appendix must not rupture as I had decided to do business in deep waters with Him. Yes, I chose to believe Him all the way.

While ruminating over the events of the past few weeks, on all appendectomies done, our visits to the hospital and the individual recuperation times, a trend was obvious. I wish my siblings were on the same page of faith with me, I wish I knew as much as I do today back then - none of them would have undergone that minor surgery because God showed up for me and He remains impartial to all who call on Him.

Certain requests made by faith and based on His word especially by a young believer that I was then, God was bound to honour. I eventually dozed off having committed all into His hands through supplication and giving of thanks. I was and still am so persuaded that once faith is intact, God will always remain committed and surely honour childish and simple acts when done in faith.

One incidence that I still laugh at was my defiance at the doctor's orders. Before we left the hospital that day and prior to my intended minor surgery, I was instructed to abstain from solid food from 6pm that evening as the surgery would be done early the next day. On arrival at home, I sauntered into the kitchen and spoke to God quietly saying, `Father, to show you that I have faith for my healing, I'm not going to take pap or any other liquid like Dr Onajin suggested, rather, I will cook rice now and eat with chicken till I'm filled. I know You will take care of this pain`.

So, with assurance of answered prayers through faith, I cooked and ate. After all, I had prayed in Jesus' name. So, before my parents both returned from work, I made Jollof rice (a favourite of many Africans especially people from Nigeria, made of rice colourized with tomato paste and spices).

My mom had insisted I passed the night in her room so she could monitor me through the night in case the pain increased; and so, I did. In the early hours of the next morning around 5am I was suddenly roused from sleep. I cannot tell if it was a vision or trance; I just knew it was real and not just a dream. It's an experience that remains indelible in my memory till date and has been a bedrock that greatly enhanced my faith. I grew a boldness to believe God for anything after that incidence. A kind of faith that grew in leaps and bounds and became contagious to as many as would pay attention to me. It taught me that a believer can believe God for anything and everything. I became so confident that the same God of old exists and can still do wonders even today. The conviction that He never came late but would always show up on time was affirmed. By this single act, I learnt that He is close to those that believe and call on Him and He is interested in every affair of our lives.In that visitation or vision, I opened my eyes and saw two heavenly beings come through from the roof top into my mom's room where I had slept right beside her. It was like the roof suddenly became transparent and accessible as they just came through without any opening or breakage.

They were so brilliantly white, humongous in size and their presence was overwhelming. It was like I was electrified to the bed at their appearance; my whole body became numb though I could see and hear all that was taking place. I didn't have the strength to speak and did not even have an idea of what to say but I was conscious and could take note of all around me.

One of these angels held something that looked like a shiny curved sword in the shape of an arc. He then stretched his hand and pressed this curvy metal across my belly twice. While it penetrated my stomach area, the experience was kind of vibrating as I lay still on the bed. Though I witnessed all that happened clearly, I could not move or say a word. I then heard the voice of one of the angels clearly speaking to me saying:

"THE SPIRIT OF HIM WHO RAISED JESUS FROM THE DEAD HAS QUICKENED YOUR MORTAL BODY".

Romans 8vs11 says, *"And if the Spirit of Him who raised Jesus from the dead is living in you, he who raised Christ from the dead will also give life to your mortal bodies because of His Spirit who lives in you"*.

The words reverberated like echoes of many waters.

Then, they were gone as fast as they came and I opened my eyes after that experience. It took a while to grasp what had just taken place. On full realization, I started to give thanks. God had intervened in my situation and reached out to me with healing. He did it on time too! I had a heavenly surgery which sealed up my appendectomy. I was so overwhelmed by that visitation. Heavenly intervention through angelic visitations are real!

My earnest admonition for every reader desiring a miracle in any aspect is the need to grow our faith till the point of being able to believe God for anything, even the impossible.

Later that day in the hospital, I was examined again by the same doctor but I showed no sign of pain anymore. However, she wasn't convinced. So she started questioning me

"But you felt pain yesterday; how come you don't feel it anymore? Are you sure it's really gone?"

I affirmed I was alright.

"I know you don't want to undergo this surgery but it's nothing, it heals quickly".

"I'm okay doctor, I don't need an appendectomy." I reaffirmed.

"Well then, let us get a second opinion. We can't afford your appendix rupturing suddenly. I will give you a note to my doctor friend in Surulere."

An appointment was booked for emergency checks at the intended hospital. At the other hospital, the doctor recommended, urine and faeces samples were taken for tests.

I can't recall specifically how long it took, but eventually, my father later received a call saying it appears there were some irregularities but that my body system seemed to have corrected whatever it was.

A friend had once asked if I ever felt any pain thereafter or what would have been my reaction if the pain returned. Well, I would have believed God all over again. However, I'm fully persuaded that whatsoever the Lord doeth, it shall be forever! I'm free and I'm free forever. Till date and to His glory, I remain free of appendicitis.

When the reality dawned on my parents that I had been healed by God, they willingly honoured my invitation to worship at that church where I was taught to believe God for healing.

And we praise God for all things!

Chapter 3

~

Graduation

D AILY, I LEARNED TO WALK WITH THE LORD and regularly there were new discoveries, more knowledge to acquire and always new levels to attain. Just when I taught I was becoming knowledgeable, I would realise there was always something new to learn.

Most importantly, there were so many adjustments to make in this walk with God. He has a standard that could not be compromised. As the word came and as I developed in my personal communion, the Holy Spirit regularly revealed issues I needed to work upon. Although many are not convinced about or don't understand restitution and therefore think it is archaic; for me, restitution was part of my personal package.

There were some rebukes (not very palatable), but grace was available to amend such ways in my walk with Him. Often, I struggled with having to change and adjust to some things that were tough; but as I yielded, help came in form of grace.

Oh! I remember His grace, I remember His mercy. I remember all He has brought me through.

Regularly we were taught and engaged in early morning cries at my fellowship where we would go out in the early hours of the morning with public address systems and preach to fellow hall mates who were still in bed.

At other times, we would dash off as early as 5.00am to the chapel of resurrection for prayer meetings. And oh! What sweet hour of prayers they were! I would give anything to undergo such days again.

Giving my life to Christ as a youth and undergraduate on campus was one of the best phases of my life. I will forever remain grateful to the Lord Jesus for reaching out to me at that time.

The importance of personal quiet time was emphasized and the need to listen for His voice daily was taught repeatedly. A song I learnt from those fellowship days and which still keeps me on is a very deep song that I just need to hear every time to fire me up:

Come Oh Lord and fill my heart

Lord I've come to seek your face

I want to know

The ways of your glory

Come oh Lord and fill my heart

One early morning, I had finished observing my quiet time as taught by the brethren and decided to be quiet in His presence. Then, the Holy Spirit dropped a scripture in my heart. It was Proverbs 31v30 (NLT):

"Charm is deceptive, and beauty does not last; but a woman who fears the Lord will be greatly praised."

As I meditated on this verse all through the day, I wondered if there was any aspect in which I had vain glory. I prayed that He would fill my heart with His reverential fear and cause my ways to please Him always. Little did I know that the Lord was warning me ahead of an incident that would shake as well as strengthen my faith in Him.

Combining my academics with fellowship activities gave life better meaning on campus. At this point, it's worth mentioning that my first-degree study wasn't quite a smooth sail. As a matter of fact, it was laden with struggles, but it further built my total dependence on God.

It was now close to our first semester exams. After lectures, I would normally stay behind to read in my department as I found the University library quite far and full of distractions.

On this fateful day, I walked into a senior lecturer who requested for my help in collating results of final year students. I respectfully told him I had a lot to catch up on from my class work with tons of assignment deadlines to meet but that I would be willing to help the next day if that was ok. He said it was and that he would send for me.

I completely forgot about that incident until he reminded me well over two years later. My mind must have been beclouded with my work load and the fast approaching exams then.

As we commenced the second semester of second year, I realized this lecturer was taking one of my major courses. It was during our first class with him that it occurred to me that he didn't send for me as earlier agreed but I just let it go thinking he must have worked with other fellow students.

As time went on, it became obvious this lecturer always picked on me in class; I just never did anything right. I failed every assignment submitted and he would maximize every opportunity to embarrass me during lectures. And when the results were released at the end of my second year, I didn't pass this course. It was a compulsory course and a prerequisite for two of my required courses in my third year.

Well, I gave thanks for all things being armed with the mind-set that I would carry over the second-year course and brace up more for the other two ahead concurrently. Incidentally, this same lecturer was to take the other two courses!

As we continued in my third year, attending lectures taught by this lecturer became a great burden; I just never did or said anything right. He would even pick on my sitting position. On one occasion, he said to me:

"Ayeni, you are too relaxed, sit up, come on, sit up!"

One of my course mates who happened to be a close friend had once asked:

"…do you have any issue with this man?"

I honestly responded that I was oblivious of any, as I sincerely didn't know of any. Apparently, I must have been very naive not to pick the signals.

It then occurred to me to pray about the issue so I prayed and asked God for favour before this lecturer. At the end of that first semester in my third year, I narrowly passed the 200-level compulsory course with a 43% mark but failed the two compulsory courses for 300-level.

It wouldn't have been a cause for worry if these were not part of my core courses. Without passing these, registering for my final year courses would be a big deal and graduation wasn't certain.

Though the traits of a first-class student were not evident in me, it was obvious my grades could be better; at least courses taught and marked by other lecturers were proof enough.

Unfortunately, you dare not call for your papers to be re-marked; such was the system in place then.

Second semester of my third year came and went peacefully and my contact with this lecturer became greatly minimized.

Eventually, we commenced the final year and I had to really seek God concerning my graduation as I didn't want an extra semester on campus. So, being overwhelmed, I sought God earnestly. It had been a great challenge registering for my compulsory courses having failed the prerequisites the previous year.

I received a scripture in Hebrews 3 v17-19. The verses 18-19 were greatly impressed upon my heart:

¹⁸And to whom swore He that they should not enter into His rest, but to them that believed not? ¹⁹So we see that they could not enter in because of unbelief." (KJV).

In other words, the Lord was admonishing me on the need to trust Him without an iota of unbelief if I was to see His salvation in my studies.

Friend, "there remains yet a rest for the people of God", may we all find and enter into that rest in any and every season of our lives. It is pertinent to trust God even when facing seemingly impossible situations.

To my uttermost dismay, I discovered that this same lecturer was taking two of my courses again in the second semester of my final year, a compulsory and a required practical course! At this point I needed the prayers of brethren.

We started lectures again, some days were good, and others were not so good. While others had their project work and a few electives to write, I was saddled with 3 extra carry-over courses. I also decided to take on two extra elective courses all in a bid to boost my cumulative grade point average so it was a very hectic semester for me. My project work suffered some setbacks too. However, I took it one day at a time simply trusting God.

About 3 weeks to the exams, I was slowly sauntering into a lecture theatre when I bumped into this same lecturer. He stopped, looked at me and said quickly before walking away:

"Ayeni, see me in my office 8.00am tomorrow morning".

"Yes sir" was all I could respond.

My heart sank as I wondered what it was all about.

So, the next morning came. I headed early enough for my department. Whatever this man had to say, there was only one way to find out. And it's still the day the Lord has made.

As I approached his office that fateful morning, I muttered a word of prayer asking God to help me.

I knocked on the door and waited. On hearing "yes, come in", I opened and went in.

We exchanged greetings and then he asked me to take a seat. I thought I sensed an unusual warmth in his voice but sincerely couldn't place it.

Or maybe I hadn't enough time to analyse it properly.

I was the least prepared for what ensued thereafter.

He addressed me for the first time by my first name which was rather strange, as it was almost customary for lecturers to address students by their surnames. He recounted how he had approached me in my 200-level to ask for assistance and I turned him down.

"My dear, you see, I was just trying to get close so we could know each other better then." He said.

Before I could respond, he proceeded further saying he had noticed me right from my first day as a fresher at the department and how much I reminded him of his old girlfriend and that he liked me.

He said he had inquired about me and having confirmed that I was a major in that department, he knew the opportune time would come.

After that, there was this awkward silence.

Then dead silence.

And more silence and he was now smiling. This made me very uncomfortable.

A very awkward situation as I wasn't even sure of how to react. I sincerely didn't expect this or better put, I just didn't get the memo all this while.

Ho, ho, ho!

Temi is an example of those the Brazilians would refer to in Portuguese: "Nao sabe de nada, innocente" meaning 'this one doesn't know anything" or what the Nigerians will derogatorily refer to as "JJC' – "Johnny Just Come".

He then got up from his seat, with his two hands in his side pockets and started pacing around. His immaculate white shirt must have been sprayed with extra starch that morning.

As he got up, my first instinct was to bolt for the door; I tell you, Usain Bolt would willingly have handed me his medal but somehow, I managed to calm myself. It was early in the morning and the door wasn't locked anyway.

He went on further to explain that I should have picked up the signals earlier. He expected that having failed me severally and marked down my assignments, I should have "come closer" to find out why.

So, all the embarrassment, bashings and failures could be likened to the burning bush experience like the one God used to attract Moses' attention?

He then spoke in Yoruba; playing whimsically with a Yoruba rhyme that interprets thus in English:

"Even if you are brilliant, you still need to know the way"

He then added: "You need me, I need you......"

Then silence again.

I finally got that what he wanted from me all the while was an affair! And that if I agreed, in return he would grade me A's in all my courses, past and present and would even influence my grades in other courses taught by his colleagues. And that I could use his office over the weekends to study.

As he continued blabbing, the scripture in Proverbs 31:30 that I had received during my second year came back strongly:

"Charm is deceptive, and beauty does not last; but a woman who fears the Lord will be greatly praised." (NLT)

I dare not depend on any favour from this man or believe any blabbing that I was beautiful. God's fear must prevail, the Lord had taken time to prepare me ahead for this just that I was very naïve and inexperienced.

Even the Holy Ghost must have been laughing, saying

'The signs were as obvious as the writing on the wall before King Darius".

Honestly speaking, this 'Mene mene Tekel tekel' was beyond Temi. Visible to the blind and audible to the deaf. How naive can one be?

With all those heavy carry overs tailing me, I sure needed an office to study!

I simply answered him that he was my lecturer, a married man and that I was a born again Christian. In my mind, I asked myself why an uncircumcised Philistine would be of any attraction to me. But may I confess one truth? I did find him attractive physically. Not that I ever saw him in that light before the advances he made that day. He had remained the troubler of Temitope all this while. Surely, the Lord knows our weaknesses and prepares us ahead.

Funny enough, he responded that he was born again too.

As I parted with him that day, I affirmed that such would never happen as it would be a sin against the God I serve.

In response, he said "ok".

I then asked if I could leave and he nodded feigning he was reading something on his table.

Obviously, I had hurt his ego.

The issue was later raised with the prayer band leader of my fellowship. He admonished me to stay true to God and that He was a father committed to always defending His children. He then prayed with me.

Exams came and passed and the final year students had deadlines for the submission of their project work. It was a rather stressful time for me as there was so much to do in meeting deadlines.

Then news of results for certain courses started trickling in. It so turned out that I had failed the compulsory course for final year and I could only imagine the same for the other two concurrent courses from my 3rd year.

At a point, I was so heavy in my heart about the prospect of not graduating that I decided to confide in my project supervisor, a much elderly man. Though he empathised with me, my telling him only worsened the situation as word got back to the lecturer.

I managed to submit my project work and decided the best option was to leave campus lest any temptation of 'seeing' any lecturer became strong.

In any case, after collation of all results, the departmental heads would meet, then at the faculty level, before the senate seats over the final results in concluding the list of prospective graduates.

So, like Joseph before Mrs Portiphar, I ran off and headed straight for home in Lagos and immediately registered at an American baking school in Victoria Island. That was a welcomed change where I could hone my baking skills and at least take my mind off everything about school. It was such a change! I thoroughly enjoyed my baking classes and with the stress of Lagos traffic, arrival at home in the evenings was with great exhaustion.

One morning after prayers, I was drifting back to sleep and in my subconscious state, I heard the Lord asking if I would still serve Him if I didn't graduate. I quickly responded that it would be painful as He had assured me of the need to believe Him and enter into His rest but that He would remain God no matter what. After that, I had this peace flood my heart.

Two days later, I received a call from a very dear friend and course mate; saying results were out and that I should come down to Ibadan so we could go check our results. It occurred to me that whether I graduated or not, I still needed to go. So I braced up, met with my two bosom course mates and as we approached my department, you can't guess who I met!! My "burning bush" experience lecturer, the very one who had shown me the other side of Goshen for three academic years in that department. My heart missed a beat as I saw him.

He looked at me straight in the eyes and said in Yoruba, my local dialect,

"Ayeni, you escaped!"

I kept mute, trying to make sense of it all but he continued;

"I had nailed you in every sense of the word that you wouldn't graduate from this campus. That God that you are serving, just continue with Him; continue serving Him. He's really with you, congrats, you are graduating".

Without any questions and acting oblivious of past events, I just thanked him. He repeatedly said "That your God eh? Continue to serve Him O."

My course mates and I proceeded to enter the departmental secretary's office where we checked our results. Verily and truly, I had graduated with a second class lower for which I had so much relief. Spending another year in that department would have been hell. God did make a way of escape for me. I was later to learn that an elderly and senior lecturer who happened to be a Muslim suddenly took interest in my result.

He later told me he just woke up one morning and had my name impressed upon his heart as someone who must graduate. At the departmental meeting, he insisted marks must be buffed up for everyone just for me to hit pass mark for all the compulsory courses with higher units that I had records of failure.

And so, the Lord delivered me from the hand of Pharaoh that I may go forth to serve Him. I headed straight to the Chapel of Resurrection with my friends to give thanks as we all made it through.

He delivered from the snare of the fowler and my soul has escaped. Psalm 124:7 says,

Our soul is escaped as a bird out of the snare of the fowlers: the snare is broken, and we are escaped (KJV).

I immediately dedicated my youth service to Him, promising that wherever He sent me I would go for Him. Faithful God! He strategically sent me to Warri in Delta State where I served as the

Assistant zonal coordinator of the Nigerian Christian Corpers' Fellowship.

That was my primary assignment aside from being placed in an Oil & Gas Servicing Company with every ease and comfort I needed as a youth corper. It didn't end at that, six months into my service year, the company transferred me to their head office in Lagos as a contract staff.

He's ever committed when we trust Him.

Chapter 4

❦

Ovarian Cancer

I HAD SET OUT THE MONTH OF MAY 2008 to wait on the Lord, committing our relocation from Aberdeen, Scotland to Macae, Rio De Janeiro in Brazil into His hands. My husband had been transferred at work. Beyond that however, it was clear the Lord had an assignment in mind for our new location.

Periods of waiting on the Lord were always exciting times as encounters of newer depths in God and revelations were sure. However, the month of May 2008 went contrary to my expectation.

Towards the early hours of the morning of 2nd May, I suddenly woke up from my sleep with a sharp pain on my neck. On touching my neck, I remembered I had a dream. In that dream, a very massive greyish/brownish cat that targeted the right side of my neck had charged at me, bitten me and disappeared as fast as it came. On recollection of this dream I thought within me, "this waiting period is going to be glorious, the devil is mad again."

I prayed a simple prayer of faith destroying every evil deposit in my life and nullifying every plan of the evil one and simply continued as if nothing happened. Few other attacks in my dream followed subsequently which left me wondering why this devil wouldn't just appear physically if he was bold, instead of coming while I slept.

By the 14th of May, feeling consistently tired became a regular experience, which could be due to the fasting combined with other activities especially in a dehydrating environment. It was taking a toll on me but having made up my mind I would reach my goal for that month, I prayed for strength to carry through.

On the 26th of May, it was obvious something was wrong with me. I woke up and I just had to take something so I drank some tea. That was when it all started. With that cup of tea, I felt so full and almost bloated. Within a few hours, my legs started to swell. Daily I grew weaker—always tired and without strength to perform any task around the house. I mentioned this to a friend and she said, "your body must be retaining fluid."

A senior missionary friend called a few days later and asked if all was well. He must have asked about three times before I told him I was a bit 'strong' and needed some rest. He told me he had a prompting to call and he prayed with me over the phone. The swelling on my legs went down but I stooled all through the night.

The following day, an aunt from Kent, London called asking why she had not heard from me in a while. When I explained that I wasn't feeling to well, she pried further and one thing led to another and that led to my recounting about the dream. She immediately rebuked me for keeping quiet all this while. She gave an instance of a sister who had been shot an arrow in her dream and died of cancer a few weeks later. She prayed with me that day.

The days rolled by and June came but my health deteriorated. Having visited the medical practice in my area thrice in June, they kept advising me to drink more water and that my body system would take care of whatever it was.

Spring came quickly and on one of those early mornings, I became so weak. So on my husband's insistence, we found our way to the accident & emergency centre of the Aberdeen Royal Infirmary. We were told that since I could still move around on my own, it was nothing life threatening.

On a return visit to the medical practice and at my insistence, samples of blood were taken for blood works. By now, my stomach was really bloated and could pass for a four months' pregnancy. My husband had to take over all the affairs of the home including school runs and all domestic affairs as I was too weak to even climb the stairs at one go. He was also running out of time as he was already overdue to resume work in Brazil.

Blood, faeces and urine samples were collected for all kinds of tests imaginable. All through this period, I experienced insomnia, constant headache, aches all over, general weakness with loss of appetite. Lying in bed was only possible on one side as there was pain on the lower side of my left abdomen. Menstruation was for only two days and it was always brown and dry with pains. Regularly, there was this feeling of acid or bile rushing into my mouth after feeling like my stomach was being whirled around with a metal wire. Stooling was a normal occurrence with no appetite for food. If I took a cup of tea, I would be so full for the rest of the day. I was pale, gaunt and with a bloated stomach—it was certain something was wrong.

After six weeks, it dawned on my husband and I that he had to make his first trip to Brazil for a quick handover. His predecessor was eager to move on to his next location for another role. We reckoned he couldn't continue giving excuses at his work place.

I had learnt in my Christian work to endure pain, pray for strength and always rise up to the challenge. I assured him the children and I would be fine in his absence; it was meant to be a short trip anyway and we were positive I would get better.

On the 30th of June, a call came through from the medical practice saying the test results were out and that my blood had been infected; there were traces of thalassemia and that my protein globulin was high as a result of fighting an undetected infection. It was advised I check into the Royal infirmary immediately. I requested for some days to sort the children pending my husband's return. My husband was called back from Brazil and immediately he came in, we all drove to the hospital.

I was then admitted and after series of tests were carried out I was transferred to three wards consecutively with each saying they could not diagnose what was wrong. A sense of panic began to set in. An experience I still chuckle at was with an Indian doctor who conducted the first scan. He screamed in his accent, "Water, water, massive volume of water, too much water".

Of course, with a swollen tommy like mine, something had to occupy the space.

On the morning of July 8 while still on admission and awaiting diagnosis, I woke up with a song in my spirit

Call Him Jesus (2ce)
The lover of my soul has given me Joy (2ce)

The song kept coming and it overwhelmed me that morning. I wasn't just singing; it was an outburst of pure joy! For no apparent reason, I was just joyous! While lying on my bed trying to meditate, the group of doctors – about seven of them walked in for their usual ward round. They asked me to come with them into the consulting room. By their countenance and extra formality, one could tell the news wasn't a palatable one.

On entering the consulting room, I met three doctors with grim faces and a nurse who started petting and patting my shoulders.

"So, Mrs. Fagade, would you like to call any family member to come give you support before we give you our findings?"

I responded that whatever it was I could handle it. No need to distract my husband from work. I was so sure God was with me.

He then went ahead to say:

"Well, em, it's a rare one in people of your age, it's common amongst women of ages 60-65; Temi, you have cancer of the ovary. The growth is as big as an apple already and that explains the pains in the left side of your abdomen…."

He went on and on.

Seeing the smile on my face, he asked me if I heard him correctly.

I responded with an affirmation and added that I happen to be a different breed and that all was going to be well with me. I wish he could discern spiritually what I meant but he obviously didn't get the memo.

It brought some level of relief to me knowing at least there was a diagnosis. The mystery phase was done with; cancer with a name, the size of an apple. And apples are meant to be eaten.

While walking out of the room, a sudden feeling of being very special overwhelmed me and I realized God was going to be glorified again. Having experienced divine healing back in my university days, the full persuasion that He was going to show up was very strong. You see, the Lord never allows anything come our way if He hasn't prepared us for such experience.

On my return into the hospital ward, fellow patients wanted to know what was said. We had all become friends and I was referred to as 'happy lass' due to my regular humming and singing.

'Oh, nothing really, the doctor was just explaining some medical terms to me,' I responded.

At that moment in time, the enemy spoke in my heart, "Did you hear well? Are you okay? They said cancer and you said it is nothing really; it's a terminal disease you know."

For a minute, my faith was shaken as the full consequences dawned on me. I sent text messages to two senior friends in the faith, giving them the doctor's report.

It was just logical to desire leaving the hospital that Friday as nothing was to be done over the weekend anyway. Apart from the various tests undergone, no medication whatsoever was being administered so exchanging the hospital environment for home was a welcome change. On pleading with the doctor for a discharge, he obliged requesting for my return as soon as they get in touch.

My husband and children came to pick me up and while we conversed, I relayed the doctors' diagnosis to my husband. He immediately rejected it and asked to speak with the doctors. He automatically "graduated" from the medical school that day and argued with them over possibilities. He questioned the possibility of fibroid; on his insistence, a scan was done and some of the water in my bloated stomach was drained with a long syringe and taken for further analysis. After the draining, my stomach size went down a bit.

In a vision that night, I saw a bald-headed lady sitting in a wheel chair looking lean and gaunt, like a withered vegetable. A closer look at the face revealed it was the enemy's picture of me. To this, constant screaming, rejection and confession of scriptures came to my aid. I regularly made loud declarations that the word of God is working for me, in me and on my behalf anytime that image appeared.

Because I had earlier been advised to increase my water consumption but saw no improvement in my health, I decided to call a doctor friend in Nigeria and share my experience. He chided me for going on prolonged fasting, he diagnosed my system must have been releasing some acidic substance and recommended antibiotics which my sister bought in Nigeria and sent to me in Aberdeen.

On getting home after receiving the news from the doctors in Aberdeen Royal Infirmary, I called that doctor friend in Nigeria again. While trying to explain things to him, he cut me short and gave me the revelation he had while he prayed for me.

The summary was that it was cancer and that I should not try to reject treatment. He counselled that I cooperate with the doctors to start chemotherapy immediately. "Temi, I hope you know I'm not just a friend and doctor but a man of God, so I know what I'm saying here". After appreciating him profusely, I requested that nothing relating to this issue be mentioned to my parents. And I prayed my confidentiality would be respected.

You see, despite his meaning well from the medical perspective, one had a choice of choosing between fact which in this case is medical belief or Truth, which is what the word of God declares over the situation. It was just a choice of choosing which report to believe. Faith in the word must prevail!

So, that night that I arrived home, we commenced administering of the holy communion. And so it was for many nights on end; we would pray neutralizing every deposit of the enemy and take communion.

My senior friend would regularly call from Manchester and inject words of faith into me over the phone. He once said to me, "Beloved, the One that has never lost a battle is on your case."

During the day, I sang hymns and my favourite then was:

Standing on the promises of Christ my King
Through eternal ages, let His praises ring
Glory in the highest I will shout and sing
Standing on the promises of God

And at night it was communion. Some days I had strength and at other times I was weak but my faith was being charged up daily. I was associating with the right set of people and guarding my heart from being affected. That was the first great lesson I learnt! The mind must never be affected no matter what, because the battle is in the mind. The Lord told Joshua, "Be Strong and Courageous…"

Have I not commanded you? **Be strong and courageous. Do not be afraid;** *do not be discouraged, for the Lord your God will be with you wherever you go (Joshua 1:9).*

Being courageous simply means having the ability to disregard fear. So in the midst of it all, I chose to disregard fear despite the pains and the unpleasant news.

The essence of the shield of faith we claim is to quench every fiery dart (be it in the thought realm or declarations from persons) of the enemy no matter how subtle; the shield is effective.

I recall one day when I needed help at home and called up a dear friend. She came over and on seeing me, she burst into tears and said, "This must be the enemy at work." Her disposition was far from encouraging and led to my resolve not to confide in anyone again. Better to be envied than to be pitied, the Lord would come through for me surely.

There were days when fear of the dark greatly overwhelmed my heart as night came; thoughts of making it through till the next day registered fear. And at dawn, while gently opening one eye after the other brought reality that I'm still alive. The lyrics of this song made better sense and more understanding in gratitude to the Preserver of my life and soul:

Whenever I see another breaking of the day,
I say thank you Lord, thank you Lord….

Towards the end of July, it became obvious my husband had to resume work in Brazil. I had to consider these options—Do I go to Nigeria for chemotherapy where help could easily be available with the children? Or relocate to Dartford with an aunt in U.K? And will medical care be available? There was also the option of inviting someone over from Nigeria to stay with us in Aberdeen while my husband resumed in Brazil. But sound counsel prevailed. My husband and I decided we would all move to Brazil so we could all be together and he could concentrate better at work. I correctly understood there was strength in the power of agreement between a man and wife.

My immediate younger sister decided to visit from Nigeria to see me. My three siblings were all aware of what was happening but I insisted my parents must not be told.

After the draining of water from my tummy, sincerely I felt a bit better. Friends in Aberdeen were all commenting about "my pregnancy" due to the protracted belly and my frail appearance. One of them said, "This pregnancy is dealing with you." Another said, "Tope, this pregnancy must be twins; the tummy shot out so fast". Yet another asked where delivery would likely be.

At all these, I always smiled as they commented, but inwardly I spoke to God, sometimes with tears. At a time, wearing the flowing African kaftan became my most frequent outfit in order to disguise by hiding the bloated stomach.

My baby sister, sent a book to me titled "Rescued from Destruction" by Mama Faith Oyedepo. It was like cold water to my thirsty soul; healing became more believable and I was assured that my case was not beyond His power. He supplied every need per time. God is too faithful to fail!

We were then set for the trip to Brazil. The doctors were not pleased with the information that my family was due to relocate to Brazil. They paid me a visit at home to speak with me on the need to commence chemotherapy. They advised at least I stay for further tests and observations. They called repeatedly on the phone, but we maintained our stand.

After a while, I started experiencing shortness of breath and was always gasping for air to the extent that staying in an enclosed place for a long time became an issue. On one Sunday as we drove to church in Aberdeen, I started gasping for breath and requested for all windows to be wound down.

Another visit at the hospital revealed water was gathering in my lungs so air wasn't circulating as it should. "The oxygen level had gone down" or so they said.

On the doctors' insistence and in preparation for the long flight to Brazil, I had a final check of my oxygen level a day before we left Aberdeen. The lady doctor checked all and gave me aspirin for the flight. A letter of discharge stating I wilfully decided to leave against medical advice and a brief description of my medical history was included.

I recall vividly the doctor saying to me, "It is better you stay here and go through treatment. You think you are well physically but clinically you are not. When you crash, you will crash big, cancer is not a small thing, all your clinical results reveal this. Honestly, I am truly scared for you." Mixed feelings brought a smile to my face at her genuine concern. With an intention to keep in-touch, I requested for her email address. For me, there was no crashing as God would come through. The one that has never lost a battle was on my case.

As we got into the car on our way home, I looked around the hospital car park where we were. It was mid-day, supposedly summer but spring was very much prevailing in the air; the doctor's words reverberated and re-echoed in my mind. I took a long and very deep breath. This is it, decision taken.

Silence was heavy in the car as we drove back home.

After a while, my husband looked at me and I just let it out at that moment.

I busted out crying, "Did you hear her? She said, "When I crash, I'm going to crash big!"

On true reflection and confession, her words really got to me and made me shed tears. And then again, the enemy came and said:

"Do you remember the song – "my head, my shoulders, my knees, my toes?" Well, it started from your leg, your stomach, now your lungs and very soon it will be your brain, by then you're finished".

At such times, I would scream out rejecting such thoughts and confessing scriptures. Oh, the Word works!

Who is it that sayeth a thing and it cometh to pass when the Lord has not said it? Who can command things to happen without the Lord's permission? (Lamentations 3:37, KJV)

It shall not stand, neither shall it come to pass.

Let us go up against Judah, and vex it, and let us make a breach therein for us, and set a king in the midst of it, even the son of Tabeal: *⁷ Thus saith the Lord God, It shall not stand, neither shall it come to pass* (Isaiah 7:6-7, KJV).

I choose life, I choose health.

The number of my days HE will fulfill.

There shall nothing cast their young, nor be barren, in thy land: the number of thy days I will fulfill (Exodus 23:26, KJV).

With a holy boldness, I cried to the Lord that night not only for healing but the gift of healing, I begged Him to compensate double for all this trouble.

Return to your fortress, you prisoners of hope; even now I announce that I will restore twice as much to you (Zecharaiah 9:12).

I was given a scripture just before we left Aberdeen; – 1 John 5v4,

For everyone born of God overcomes the world. This is the victory

that has overcome the world, even our faith.

This scripture was the greatest chemotherapy ever needed! It must have fired life back into me. That aunt in Kent also sent to me communion elements which I greatly appreciated and took along to Brazil.

Our travel route on Air France was from Aberdeen – Paris – Rio. The journey to Brazil should take 11.45hours from France. We were billed to leave Aberdeen on a Friday but landed in Rio de Janeiro on Sunday morning.

The airplane used by Air France that fateful Friday was small so my family could not be accommodated on the flight and we passed the night in a hotel. Early Saturday morning, we flew to Amsterdam but my family was not permitted to fly to France by the immigration as we did not have the required EU connecting visa. Interesting that despite possessing UK work visas, we were still denied.

We then had to go back to London to fly to Paris. I should have realized that even the gates of Brazil were co-operating with the forces of darkness as my husband jokingly said to me at Amsterdam, "It's amazing we are being denied here, I passed this same route just a few weeks ago from Brazil with ease."

Eventually, the gates of Brazil and every everlasting door had to be lifted as the King of Glory came through.

Lift up your heads, you gates; be lifted up, you ancient doors, that the King of glory may come in (Psalm 24:7).

We were compensated for all the problems and upgraded to first class. The stress at the airports was more than enough to wear us all out as we slept all through the eleven hours' flight. There was no need whatsoever for walking around or for consumption of water or aspirin till we landed in Rio de Janeiro.

Hallelujah!

Chapter 5

~

The Diagnosis

AFTER WE SETTLED IN THE HOTEL AND my husband resumed at work, we decided to visit a standard hospital in Rio de Janeiro for a second opinion. The renowned hospital was a 3-hour drive from Macae, our base city. On getting to the hospital, I was examined and immediately admitted to undergo series of tests and examinations.

My husband and the kids had to return to Macae without me. My kids were left at the mercy of a babysitter in the hotel while my husband worked. The kids could not even communicate with the baby sitter as the lingua franca in Brazil is Portuguese. But in the midst of it all, the Lord gave me peace; certainly, God would take care of my children during my time on admission. Many times, our extended family got in-touch to know how we were faring in the new location. We however kept this news from them especially my parents to spare them the agony. God will still be glorified as He would come through for us.

Three doctors had been assigned to look into my case and after four days, all the tests they did were inconclusive. The ultrasound and CT scans, colonoscopy, endoscopy, biopsy, laparoscopy inclusive revealed nothing. The doctors said something was wrong because there was a thick dark "thing" covering the whole of my peritoneum; the serous membrane that forms the lining of the abdominal cavity. And for that reason, they could not see anything inside and they claimed whatever it was, was still spreading.

I was given a purgative, and was made to abstain from food and all colourized liquids, contrasts were injected into me with iodine but still the dark thickening remained.

At this point, I must confess that I didn't hand over the medical report handed to me by the doctors at the Aberdeen Royal Infirmary to the doctors in Rio. I felt it was better for them to do their own findings which I secretly believed would be different.

I was discharged a few days later, the medical team advised I would be called back after their joint meeting within the next few days. The question on my mind was "Greater One, when will this all be over?" On one of those days, I heard in my spirit:

"All the ways of the Lord are loving and faithful toward those who keep the demands of his covenant.".

I later discovered that was Psalm 25v10 which should have birthed the title for this booklet before I decided to add other life experiences to the manuscript.

A return visit to the hospital about a week later required the need for biopsy and laparoscopy conducted as my body tissue was needed for further tests. The laparoscopy involved drilling two holes near both pelvic while another was drilled through my navel so they could pass a torch through to see what was going on inside. Again, the result proved inconclusive. This news got me shattered but I never doubted that God heals. It was time also to start praying against confusion as the three doctors all had different opinions.

At this point I began to meditate and confess all sins; known, unknown, including generational sins. I even wondered within me if there was yet any restitution left undone.

A conversation with an acquaintance reminded me of the conversation Zophar and Job had. This lady had called saying intercessions were being offered on my behalf and that if there was any hidden sin I should confess in other not to hinder answers to their prayers. I was almost taking offense at these words but quickly realized taking offense could be a weapon in the hand of the enemy. Though God could decide to move in His sovereignty, another lesson here was that the prince of this world must find nothing as a foothold or for accusation; total alliance with God's words is priority.

One of the scriptures I read and that jumped at me that period was from Romans 4v20-21,

"Yet he did not waver through unbelief regarding the promise of God, but was strengthened in his faith and gave glory to God, ²¹ being fully persuaded that God had power to do what he had promised".

That was another medication for my healing. I felt like I was being held by the hand of God. I resolved to wait more patiently on Him.

Other specialists came in to see me and there were several visits to the hospital. Recalling one of such hospital visits, the first medical personnel I met got me a bit edgy. The hair on my skin stood up or maybe I was just overly sensitive. Immediately she walked in and said to me with her fluent English but with a Brazilian accent "So, this your disease, how long have you had it….?"

But before she finished her sentence I cut her short and replied, "Good day to you, I beg your pardon it is not my disease. It is a fact that my body is going through a strange occurrence but the One that has the power to remove and replace is on my case. The truth is, it is not my disease."

Though she was quick to apologize, the battle of words had to be fought and sensitivity played a big role.

On this visit, water was drained from my lungs with a long needle.

While meditating on one of those days at the hotel, it occurred to me that nothing brings you closer to your God than trouble. Pain, trials, persecution, troubles are good for me.

Little wonder the Psalmist said in Psalm 119 v71,

"It was good for me to be afflicted so that I might learn your decrees."

Though this illness was not as a result of a sin but to glorify God, I sure learnt lessons in no small measure, some of which I will treasure throughout my life's sojourn.

In the hospital, it took God to encourage me as it was just His presence with me all through. Recalling how some of the medical staff would say to me in Portuguese 'tira tudo' meaning remove everything. Trouble isolates one with God, He is truly a very present help in trouble.

I had friends and family but none except God was always present.

I had clothes but was confined to the hospital garment.

I had shoes but couldn't wear them then.

I had rooms in my house but was confined to a hospital bed.

Suddenly, the pains increased in Brazil. One of the early mornings, we started praying as the pains intensified. As my husband and I prayed on a previous occasion, he was close to tears and asked God "why us?" It should be understood he was facing challenges of work with pressure in a new environment and a different culture with a foreign language, saddled with the responsibility of fathering the children alone, and endless hospital visits with no visible light in the tunnel. I simply answered him it was because we were special. On some occasions, he did the encouragement while at other times I did.

I strongly believe that troubles and problems are bridges that take us to the land of honour. At one time or the other we must all pass through this bridge in one way or another.

I still have the letter my then 8-year-old son wrote to Jesus asking Him to heal his mom so she wouldn't have to go to the hospital all the time.

Being alone in a strange land without a place of worship and the language barrier during our early days in Brazil led us to worship online. On one of those Sunday mornings, my husband and I were online worshipping with Winners Chapel when Bishop Oyedepo said, "God's word is forever settled in heaven, it takes your own faith to settle your portion".

As I was still digesting those words, he went on further to say, "You are not a product of what you know but a product of what you know and believe".

Those words totally drenched into my spirit, soul and body. I greatly relish those words till date.

I was in and out of admission on several occasions; and on an occasion, one of the doctors suggested conducting tests for tuberculosis since water had accumulated in my abdomen and lungs earlier. I was immediately isolated and there were restrictions to who could come into my room to see me. All the hospital staff treated me like a confirmed TB patient. The doctors would come into the room with their noses and mouths all covered up and stay for a short time, the other medical personnel including cleaners and cooks avoided my room as much as possible. If necessary, they would just come in, do whatever needed to be done and hurry off.

I really wept at this treatment and understood what it meant to be ostracized. It was only natural that nobody wanted to contact tuberculosis.

Mantoux test was carried out and strangely after three days I had a very big swelling on my left arm – just above my wrist but all the other tests were negative.

So, the big question came, do I undergo treatment for tuberculosis simply because of the swelling on my arm? No coughing, my x-rays were clear but the doctor claimed there was a possibility of the TB bacteria settling in my abdomen instead of the lungs. I was again discharged; the doctors needed to have a meeting.

It was suggested that removing my womb might help to avoid further spreading of whatever it was but I bluntly refused. God can and will replace anything that needs to be fixed. I thought within me, what if I later wanted a retirement baby like father Jacob's Benjamin? Then I would have to be believe God all over again for a womb.

Having prayed and sought counsel, the only thing received was the chorus of the song by Evangelist Chris Gwamna in my spirit, it says

"The word of the Lord will not fail until Shiloh comes, until Shiloh comes".

I received another call from the hospital to come in for admission and I began to wonder what would happen next. And then, I received an email from an aunt saying it was best to commence treatment based on counsels from some medical practitioners as water was accumulating in the abdomen and lungs. I also received another call from a father figure in the faith that same day and was advised I should commence treatment.

He reassured me of being spiritually backed up while I fulfilled the medical part. He prayed with me and assured me total healing was sure even before going halfway through with the treatment.

So, having heard from two witnesses, I commenced treatment for tuberculosis. Both their spiritual stands were highly valued without which believing God all the way for His divine touch would have been my option. After all, I am a believer. Hebrews 10v35-38 admonishes believing to the end,

Therefore do not cast away your confidence, which has great reward. [36] For you have need of endurance, so that after you have done the will of God, you may receive the promise: [37] "For yet a little while, And He who is coming will come and will not tarry. [38] Now the just shall live by faith; But if anyone draws back, My soul has no pleasure in him."

Never would I hold back from trusting God to heal. The heroes of faith often did not see the fulfilment but relished in the hope of its fulfilment.

The first few days were horrible as my body reacted to the drugs and I had to return to the hospital. My body felt strange and did not welcome the drugs. What was apparently going on was that my liver was being overworked and the acid level in my body had shot up. These medications were stopped temporarily and I was given a new set of drugs to help counter the effects of the tuberculosis medications.

Then the big question came, if I really had TB, what about my husband and children. To the glory of God, they all tested negative, their lungs were all clear, their x-rays were all normal. No one had tuberculosis in the family!

By October ending (six weeks into the six months of my commencing treatment for tuberculosis), strength started to return, I could walk for longer distances, give better attention to the kids, I was not gasping for breath anymore, life was fully returning but I took things really easy. It got better with each passing day – oh the victory of the cross!

On the receipt of medical clearance to travel in December 2008, I took a trip with the children to the UK early January 2009. This trip was a welcomed change for me. In the course of this trip, we stopped by briefly in Aberdeen to see old friends.

Visiting the doctors in Aberdeen led to many medical checks over and over again. They were lost for words, they kept examining and re-examining my body as well as comparing with the information they held in their system. They asked far too many questions but I simply reminded them that God heals. I was asked to come back in another three months for further tests and a full CT scan. I returned to our new base in Brazil joyous that it was a finished work.

Subsequent visit to the UK months later by my husband revealed the hospital authorities were really waiting for my return visit. While he went for his annual check-up, the medical doctor who attended to him on sighting his surname asked if he was related to me and that the hospital had my case note pending. Whether their interest in my case was out of curiosity or genuine concern, I cannot tell.

Having completed the treatment for tuberculosis on the 28th of February, Friday the 13th of March 2009 was marked by my Brazilian Doctor (Dra Nalita B) for revised visit. I travelled down to Rio; to the Hospital called Clinica Sao Vincente; a hospital I had grown so familiar with as I visited regularly every month, sometimes forthnightly, and often weekly, depending on how the pains were. There were periods it was twice a week. A journey of three hours inbound and three hours outbound. All between July 2008 and March 2009.

Though I felt better physically, the test was to confirm the state of my system. I was a bit jittery all through my journey to the hospital and so many "what ifs" crossing my mind. I kept praying "Lord, grant me rest please, Lord, give me rest".

After four hours of intensive examination and fast-tracked test results, my doctor said 'Temi, we have compared the CD result we had in July last year when you first came in with what we have today (March 13, 2009), it's totally opposite, I have had the radiographer look too. Your system is perfectly normal, all clean and clear, your heartbeat and lungs are as new as a baby's. She raised her hands upwards and said thanks to God, Temi, I was almost getting scared for what the result would be. What I like most Temi, was your comportment towards it all, you were always smiling'.

I remember clearly her Portuguese English wherewith she always said to me on my arrival at the hospital: "Let me 'examinate' you, Temi".

And I would always correct her that the word is "examine", not "examinate". We would repeat and both laugh over this at almost every visit.

We hugged and I really shed tears being full of emotions then as I appreciated her especially for all her care (she was the only one amongst the doctors who stood with me to the end) before we parted for my return trip to my family in Macae. The Lord bless Doctora Nalita!

I cannot pen down how much financial resource was spent for all these examinations in Brazil. Oh, I celebrate the free gift of life! I celebrate the victory of the Cross!

Oftentimes, the Lord allows pains or troubles because the gain will always outweigh the pain. That is what 2 Corinthians 4v17 says,

"For our light and momentary troubles are achieving for us an eternal glory that far outweighs them all".

"We must allow Him take us through it and learn all we need to learn, never cut corners with God. In scriptures, everyone goes through trouble before glorification. Thereafter you get to your wealthy place – Psalm 66 v10-12:

> *"For you, God, tested us;*
> *you refined us like silver.*
> [11] *You brought us into prison*
> *and laid burdens on our backs.*
> [12] *You let people ride over our heads;*
> *we went through fire and water,*
> *but you brought us to a place of abundance.*

He again takes us through pains so we can always remember we owe all to Him, as humans we forget very easily; that is what Hebrews 2v1 says:

"We must pay the most careful attention, therefore, to what we have heard, so that we do not drift away".

Again, no flesh must glory in His presence else we have not truly known Him. 1 Corinthians 1v29 says, *"so that no one may boast before him".*

This flesh stinks before God. I glory only in knowing Him - Jeremiah 9v23-24:

"This is what the Lord says:
Let not the wise boast of their wisdom
or the strong boast of their strength
or the rich boast of their riches,
²⁴ but let the one who boasts boast about this:
that they have the understanding to know me,
that I am the Lord, who exercises kindness,
justice and righteousness on earth,
for in these I delight,"
declares the Lord".

Psalm 50v15 says our lives must glorify Him so we must let the glory burst forth.

"and call on me in the day of trouble; I will deliver you, and you will honour me."

God will also take us through pains so that He can judge the enemy – Deuteronomy 32v4:

"He is the Rock, his works are perfect,
and all his ways are just.
A faithful God who does no wrong,
upright and just is he".

The scriptures can never be broken. At the end of it all, I'm falling in love with Him more by the day. I have secured a new depth in Him. God showed up for me, and my case ended in thanksgiving. He did not give me as prey to their teeth.

Blessed be the LORD, who hath not given us as a prey to their teeth (Psalm124v6, KJV).

In recounting His healing power, His mercy and abundant grace towards me, I sing:

I've been changed

Healed

Freed

Delivered

I've found joy

Peace

Grace

And favour

Chapter 6

$\backsim$

A Parenting Mind

I HAVE CHOSEN TO USE FICTITIOUS names to represent the actual characters of this story for privacy reasons. "I'm sick and tired of how you control my life, I have a brain. I have the right to do anything I want to do, leave me alone and stop controlling my life! Jack's mom doesn't treat her children like you do; they do anything they want, whenever. She's a better mom than you".

Those were words I received from my first child and son roughly 9 years ago. He was barely 8 years old.

Whenever I'm confronted with discussions on challenges of raising kids in foreign cultures, those words above always reverberated through my mind. Now, I smile over that experience. You see, you only raise a child following God`s principle and that is by seeking Him personally on any and every issue. Please come down memory lane with me.

We had recently relocated to Rio de Janeiro and the rudest shock we received on arrival was that of language barrier. Those were days I wished one could have a face-to-face dialogue with Mr. Nimrod concerning his Babel Towers attempt.

While settling in, we met this European family; our kids and theirs attended the same school and we lived three houses apart. Naturally, we became family friends. Well, at least, for the sake of our children. They had arrived earlier in Brazil about three months or so ahead of us.

As my kids got closer to this neighbour's children, I felt a bit relieved that they at least had respite in the new environment we found ourselves by God`s design.

An incident that should have prepared me for what later happened had been treated with levity. But for heavenly help and His purpose a lot could have gone wrong.

One cool afternoon in the Brazilian early spring, Jack's mom walked into my house as was typical of her to visit to ask how I was doing and the following conversation ensued between us after exchanging pleasantries.

"Temi, something happened at dinner last night that I need to let you know about." Before I could respond, she continued;

"You know Jack's father has been travelling? Well, he returned late last night from his trip. He bought Jack and the girls some gifts. Jack got a Nintendo Wii which he had always desired." I listened with rapt attention, wondering where this would end.

Even my fast racing mind could not have deciphered.

"The first words that came out of Jack`s mouth as his father handed him the Nintendo was "Hallelujah, finally!" We were all surprised and wondered where he had learnt such words...."

I hadn't the faintest idea of what she was getting out so I listened more, eager to hear it all.

"We interrogated him to know where he had learnt such words and he mentioned Daniel had been teaching him some things about God and telling him stories from the Bible".

And then she looked at me intently, with this pain in her eyes and said, "Temi, we don't believe in any God; it was my husband that worked for his money and bought the items for his children; it wasn't any God".

"Please instruct Daniel to stop telling Jack such stories".

"Oh!" was the surprised response I could give.

I then politely explained to her that we were Christians and do believe in the existence of God that created the heavens and the earth and we, as the inhabitants. And that we were created to bring Him glory. She didn't seem interested in hearing me but I felt I had also established my own stand without denying my faith.

One thing was clear, I would never apologise for my faith. Having had real experiences with this God, the least I could do was affirm my faith before anyone that cared to listen.

She then changed the topic and we just moved on from there.

As the kids got back from school, I queried Daniel to know what exactly transpired and he recounted how he had been telling Jack about Bible stories during break time at school and that he seemed really interested since he had never heard such in his entire life. My son was so excited sharing this with me.

I summarised Jack's mother's visit without discouraging him directly. However, it was difficult to separate the kids as they were the only English-speaking family we had close by. As time went by, it all fizzled out of my mind. The kids took turns for after school visits.

One hot summer afternoon, the kids were on one of such visits to Jack's place.

I had reminded them that their visit mustn't exceed two hours. They know I mean what I say and that I say what I mean.

Almost 3 hours later, I suddenly realized they were nowhere in sight so I called the mother of their friends by phone to send them home.

Well, the woman still requested that they wait for some snacks she was baking but the realization of their lateness made them return running home and mumbling aloud "Oh no, we really have to go. Mommy may not allow us come here to visit again, we need to hurry."

I later realized their comments startled the lady and her children. They felt like, "What's the fuss? Why the rush? Any big deal in staying out a little longer than planned?"

On their arrival, I chided them for flaunting my orders. 'Daddy will hear about this', I had threatened.

This family's curiosity had unknowingly been aroused by that simple incident. The woman and her son took it upon themselves to interrogate my son on a regular basis. They queried him if I abuse either him or his sister through harsh punishments or beatings. She went to the extent of inspecting his body for marks as she had learnt African parents can be mean.

Though I never agreed to sleepovers, I still permitted their regular visits. Little did I know my son's heart was being poisoned toward his mom. I noticed he became a bit daring, questioning my instructions and often giving snappy answers but I sincerely attributed these to the change of environment. "Poor boy," I thought, "he's finding it difficult to settle at school, not many English speakers around; he's missing his old friends."

So, I made excuses for him. Until the day they returned late from another visit and before I could complete my sentence he busted out expressing his desire to be free because he had a brain and that his friend's mom was better than I was.

"Daniel, what did you just say?" He simply shouted,

"You heard me, I'm just tired of you controlling my life; if you pester my life, Jack's mom will take me to the police and social welfare; I'm just tired, I'm tired."

He then dashed off to his room crying.

I felt like the whole world was crashing right on me. My daughter stood in silence, having witnessed the whole scenario.

At that point, I needed to talk to someone. My husband was away on an official trip. Relating such incidence over the phone would devastate him considering he was far away. His imagination would run wild.

I thought about calling my parents however, the response from their end unanimously would be;

"Send him home to Nigeria, immediately, we will train him."

Sleep evaded my eyes that night; my heart was heavy! I felt like I had lost all. I had mentioned to his father over the phone that he was a bit naughty. I would wait till his return before divulging details. He was due back within 3 days anyway.

As I couldn't sleep, I decided to go check on him in his room. I found he was awake. Sitting by his bed, I asked why he wasn't sleeping and if he needed anything. He just stared into space without a response. Silence lingered between us for a while.

Then I asked what he was thinking, what his fears were before zeroing in on what a policeman would do on discovering you disobeyed your mother.

I then said, "Do you know what the work of a social worker is? They separate families. That means you will never see me, your dad or your sister again. Is that what you want? That we separate forever? What exactly have I done to merit that from you?"

At that point, he started crying and then opened up with many staggering conversations between him, Jack and Jack 's mom.

They had told him to annoy me and possibly record my response on a device. They went as far as suggesting he keep a knife under his pillow and that anytime I asked him to do anything he doesn't like, he should threaten to kill himself.

At that point I knew I had to call my husband and relate all. There was fire on the roof top! Not only wisdom but the situation needed a very responsible faith to handle.

Thankfully, I could inject some sense into him that night. I admonished from scriptures and sighted present examples from other families. It must have taken God for me to come down to his level in explaining the consequences. Obviously, he understood as he wept bitterly and apologized. As a mother, I was full of emotions and did shed tears too.

By the time I retired to bed, we both knew there was no school in the morning.

We spent the following day together as I just drove them around the city, we walked on the beach and had lunch in a restaurant. I took it really easy, became extra vigilant, watched every word I said while continually listening "within" for the best strategy. The best that came to my mind was to wait for their dad to return from his trip, pack my bags and that of the kids and just get out of there!

Much later that afternoon, Jack's mom came over asking why they weren't in school and wondered if all was well. I reassured her we were fine but that I had a late night and couldn't wake up early enough for school drop off.

In my heart, I felt like letting all hell loose and giving her a piece of my mind before walking her out but blessed be God for restraint. As she left, I muttered in a low tone to myself, "Lord, even this must end to my benefit, no matter what, I must win."

King David in the Bible was a man that knew his weapons very well. While others thought he needed the sword and armoury to confront Goliath, David knew all it would take to bring down his adversary was that sling and a stone.

So after dropping them off in School the next day, it was pertinent to pray a prayer that would not go into storage but that would receive answers immediately. As I settled down, it occurred to me it wasn't the story telling kind of prayer but an asking prayer that I needed. So I resolved to just ask what to do in this situation. Not forgetting to mention that I asked with such agony in my heart. My heart was bleeding as a mother.

I hadn't stayed for more than 1 hour in His presence when the answer came. I was led to Exodus 3:12 and the very last phrase popped out boldly at me. "*. . . on this same mountain, Ye shall worship me*" (KJV).

Oh what joy, oh what peace! As I meditated on that, I felt the burden lift. I came out a different person. My countenance was greatly lightened. Hasn't He promised to contend with those that contend with me and that He would save my children in Isaiah 49:25?

But the LORD says, "The captives of warriors will be released, and the plunder of tyrants will be retrieved. For I will fight those who fight you, and I will save your children (NLT).

No need to run away; I'm a believer, not a doubter. I'm an overcomer always. The earth is the Lord's and the fullness thereof says Psalm 24 v1,

The earth is the Lord's, and everything in it, the world, and all who live in it.

I refused to be uprooted, as I realized He planted me there for a reason!

So I got my kids involved in extra activities after school such that "visitation" became virtually impossible. We went from swimming to basketball to Kumon lessons. Sometimes we just walked around the shopping malls. Weekends were busier as we toured near and far.

Precisely a month after, Madam Sally (Jack's mum) walked over to my house really sad and in a low tone said to me,

"Oh Temi, can you believe this? We have been transferred back to our home country. It's even less than seven months! We were just settling in. And to imagine I'm going back during winter!! Harsh winter. I was beginning to love it here . . ." She went on and on while I kept repeating the same words, "Oh, what a pity, what a pity."

After she left, I leave you to imagine my thoughts and feelings. I am so glad I didn't raise my voice to fight that woman earlier. Hear me, beloved: Silence is a great weapon - Selah. Let the Lord handle your battles, always, at all times!

I sent a message to my husband at work asking him to call when he was less busy and as I related to him he said to me, "Mama Mia! He uprooted them for you."

I laughed and replied, "Don't mess with Temi, I'm here on a mission!"

So again I say:

Lord you have done all things well!

I did learn a few but deep and unforgettable lessons from that experience some of which I'm willing to share here:

Firstly, it is pertinent for all parents to know and maintain their family values. Apart from the fact that no two families are the same, no environment or foreign culture should make you lose or compromise what you believe, uphold and practise as a family in God. As a matter of fact, allowing foreign culture to have an impact on how you raise your children brings confusion to them. So, as long as it doesn't contradict the word of God, hold on tightly to them.

Joshua was a man of great convictions such that he declared:

'...as for me and my house, we will serve the Lord' (Joshua 24:15b).

In your household, never compromise the place of family altar, just because you have visitors. Whoever comes into your home must comply or at least, respect your family values. It builds confidence in the children. When you raise your family in line with God's principle, He is committed to helping you as a family.

I do have my reservations about the sleepover culture and discourage it at any and every opportunity. They can stay and play with friends all day but what has night to do with it? Without infusing any negative thoughts, Christian parents must realize a lot of activities occur in the night season. We must be sensitive not to take everything at face value. Lest the enemy takes advantage of us. It may call for assertiveness. Be mindful of the families our children are exposed to. They can undo what we have used years to build. Be reminded that God gave these children as wards to care for; we can always run back to Him for counsel on how to raise them correctly in times of difficulty. The point is, scriptures are available for this, however the enemy can still make attempts to snatch them or basically to get back at the believing parent. We depend on the only wise God for wisdom on how to counter any such attacks of the enemy.

Let me register a concern here; whether at home or in diaspora, we all look for respite as raising a child is tough work, we must remember a few things. We are accountable to God for how these children turn out.

There exists that glorified baby sitter called tablets that parents purchase for their children; research has shown that a child you expose early to the mercy of such gadget will likely grow without feelings. Children need to learn sweetness and love from the parents. One painful truth is that though many things can wait, the growth of children can't as they grow so fast. The Lord graciously blessed me with another baby boy after 13 years of having my last daughter. I do not take this gift for granted and with that mindset that they grow fast, I consciously make efforts to be available for him and this I will continually do by His grace.

A sad incidence I learnt about from a friend was how the child innocently got addicted to pornography and subsequently, masturbation while mom and dad hustled to make money. This little boy had confessed that mommy was always busy so he had no choice but to turn to TV to pass time and had stumbled on this channel while flipping the remote control. What they were "doing" caught his attention. One thing led to another and he decided to "try it out" secretly until masturbation became a daily habit of his once he wakes in the morning. Sadly, the enemy crept in early and captured this innocent soul at age 10.

Though the parents' absence may not always be responsible, when we are constantly unavailable, the enemy offers options to our children. The pain of this wounded mother is unquantifiable however the addiction has eaten deep into this boy because **while men slept, the enemy came and sowed tares** *(Matthew 13 v 25)*.

Parents, especially mothers must develop spiritual sensitivity that are high in a bid to detect arrows from the enemy. There is a call for greater sacrifice on the part of the mother as they have been called to "nurture". When a man and his wife walk in unity of purpose and mind, especially on raising children, it is much more difficult for the enemy to penetrate.

It is also important to correct on the trivial. I once heard the saying that you don't correct on everything. My take is, correct as much as possible but in love. It takes a lot of repitition before words sink into a child, but we must not faint. It is tough work but God will be grateful. I still wonder how prophet Eli missed it in raising Hophni and Phinehas. And I wonder why there was no mention of Mrs Eli. However, the Lord held Eli responsible (1Samuel 2: 12-36).

Moses was also an absentee father. He was busy doing God's work at the expense of attending to his family. It took his father-in-law to help set his family in order. If God knew the mother could do it alone, there would have been no need for the father figure and vice versa.

The life of Lot revealed his words didn't carry much weight before his children and sons-in-law. Perhaps his child raising skills were weak or he lived a double standard life in Sodom and Gomorrah. The question is, to which of the above categories do you belong? Or can God boldly say of you like father Abraham that you are *a man that will command your family after God?* (Genesis 18v19). May grace be supplied henceforth in fulfilling this noble assignment for God.

And of course, the most potent weapon is the weapon of prayer. It is pertinent for one to really know this God. Certain happenstances in our lives will require trusting God fully to fight for us. It would require absolute trust in God to lead us and show up in our situation.

He is very interested in all that concerns us and He loves it when we involve Him. Very little is achieved if we take actions just by ourselves. Consciously, we must learn to depend on Him. Little wonder the Bible says in the book of Daniel that they that know their God shall be strong and do exploits. Beyond going to church, our relationship with God must be real and on-going.

Another important aspect is learning to ask questions in prayer (*Ask and ye shall receive...* Matthew 7v7, KJV) and learning to "listen." Listening is a very important aspect of prayers.

Friends, at whatever point we are in raising of God's heritage in our care, there's hope because help is always available in God. No situation is too late for Him to correct. He instituted the family and knows how best to fix any issue. Let's just come to him admitting our mistakes and ignorance in raising these ones by asking for wisdom. As we earnestly seek His face, the God we expect will suddenly show up at His temple. For every trouble, He can and will render double. When God takes His time to fight for a child of His, He fights big!!

Be friends with your children; play, gist and relate with them—it does not take away your role as a parent. A child you do not make out time for is already lost and may never open up to you during difficult times especially at the formative age. Such a child will end up learning basic norms of importance in life from the outside world. They need to know they can trust you and that you will understand and always be there for them. As selfish as it may sound, when I announced I was pregnant to my two teenagers, the first question my son asked was, "So, who's going to be taking me for basketball? Now the love will be divided…"

This above phrase depicts a longing for attention and that yearning to know they occupy an important place in your heart irrespective of their age. Every child needs to be shown and reassured of that love especially from mothers who "nurture" in every sense of the word. There is a need to affirm to them the special place each child holds in the heart of the mother irrespective of how many children she has. The bulk of the assignment lies with the mother who can continually draw strength from the double-breasted God.

Chapter 7

~

An Interesting Sojourn

"SO, YOU MEAN WE AREN'T YET SURE on where we are moving to...?"

"No, Bibi, but it will come clear soon. When the Lord gives us a clear direction, I'll let you know, ok? I need to go shopping now".

"But wait, Mommy, honestly, I'm tired of just moving around, let`s just go back to Aberdeen and settle forever. It`s tiring being the new kid at school every time......"

"Is Aberdeen your hometown? Well, I've told you we are sojourners here on earth. Father Abraham moved around a lot more during his time – wherever the Lord bid, he went".

"But I'm sure father Abraham didn't have many boxes to move around. He didn't pack and unpack. He didn't have to study or change schools. He only had animals and he had lots of servants to help with stuff around".

"You are right and don't forget, father Abraham also lived in tents whether it was harshly cold or in the scorching heat of some deserts. You have lived in houses with roofs over your head all this while. And you relocate in airplanes, not on foot or donkey backs. Fortunate you are. We remain pilgrims on a journey, remember? I need to go now".

This conversation transpired between my first son and I precisely November 2010. He was almost 10 then.

Wondering what led to this? Well, here's my story to His glory:

It was a lazy, hazy morning in a small city called Macae and though unduly extended, winter was gradually giving way to spring in October. The Brazilian spring called Primavera in Portuguese had been much awaited by all. I could feel the tussle as spring tried to usher itself in while forcing winter out of the scene.

That fateful morning, my husband had lamented about the recent stress at work. And then he shared a dream he had. We prayed against any evil occurrence. However, it came to pass a week later.

That fateful Friday noon in October, he called me from work, sounding rather low. Typically, I encouraged him.

Again, we spoke around 4.00pm.

At about 6.00pm, he called again and we conversed. He said, "I just received a call to come for a meeting scheduled for 7.00pm at the base…. this is it Temi. I know… I feel it…."

And I responded, "Whatever it is, just go through. Our God reigns over all. Receive strength. See you soon".

I needed to get my mind busy so I walked past the kids watching TV and as I sauntered into the kitchen, my pulse rate noticeably had increased.

I started dinner and just as I was rounding up, he called again. And a short dialogue ensued between my husband and I.

His voice was weary as he spoke.

"It's happened Temi, I just received the letter and I've signed acknowledgement. Its over... Need to go pack my personal belongings from the office..."

He left it hanging so I picked it up.

"It's ok, please come home, we still need you. We will go through this together and we will all be fine. Or do you want me to come over...?"

But he had hung up.

I leaned against the wall for a minute with my head looking up. "Dear Lord! Please grant us the grace for this. And it's just two days to his birthday!"

Then I called my two kids into the kitchen and gently broke the news to them as I stroked my daughter's hair.

And she said, "So you mean Daddy doesn't work here anymore? And now, what? We get to leave Brazil...? Where to now?" And more questions from both of them.

"Shall we just pray and thank the Lord? Remember we are to give thanks in all situations?" I said.

And the three of us got down on our knees in the kitchen and thanked God for the news.

As we heard his car drive into the garage, we all rushed out to welcome him. Sadness hung around.

We hugged him and then silence. Then he regaled with the details.

I requested to see the dismissal letter:

"motive: without prejudice"

I served dinner.

I could see the kids had questions as they kept stealing glances in their father's direction.

Then my eight-year-old daughter blurted out:

"So, Daddy, what are you going to do now? Be a fireman like you had always wanted to…...?"

"Let's just eat and talk about that later, ok?" I chipped in.

But her dad responded with a smile before continuing to pick on his food. I looked closely at him and discovered grey hair was fast breaking forth.

I could bet his worries was not just about getting another job but being fired was a big blow to him and without prejudice as his dismissal letter stated.

On the next morning, a Saturday, calls tripped in from wives of colleagues. Some to confirm what happened, others to empathize. Bad news sure spreads like wild fire.

Call after call, I responded cheerfully without a mention of what happened until a lady asked me directly:

"Temi, is it true...?"

"Is what true, dear?"

"That your husband was relieved of his duties yesterday? That's a big blow, you know. And everybody believes there was no basis for it, they all say he was so professional and he had greatly improved the segment revenue since he assumed that role......."

And I responded without cutting her directly.

"My darling, that company was just a channel, the source remains heaven. Painful but we are not moved. God will sort him out. All is well and I do appreciate your call".

I answered a few other calls.

Sincerely, the atmosphere was becoming gloomy around us. But I remembered joy must always be present if God's hand was to be activated in this situation. He inhabits the praises of His people (Psalm 22:3), not their moroseness and last, I checked, a merry heart doeth good like medicine (Proverbs 17:22).

And then an idea occurred to me that Saturday evening.

The next day was his birthday and I had thought we would all eat out in a restaurant after church service. Instead, we would have a party in the house to celebrate promotion! A praise party it would be. We would invite all friends and colleagues. And with lots to eat and drink.

Oh! What an odd, weird idea as I thought for a minute. Isn't it wise to conserve on any spending in this prevailing circumstance? Shouldn't we just lie low and re-strategize at a time like this? But the more I thought about it, the more it made sense and I felt a leap of joy. We withhold not, even this act will lead to further increase. Party, Praise, thanksgiving and make merry WE SHALL!

This is an inspired desire, surely it will bring good.

So around 8.00pm that Saturday evening, I announced to my husband and kids that we were having friends over for dinner to celebrate daddy's birthday. And with a corner of an eye, I watched out for reactions.

I noticed some excitement on their faces and my husband responded with a smile. He had suddenly become a man of very few words.

And then invites were sent out via text messages for the praise/promotion party.

So, for the first time in years, I did something really weird. While they all headed for church service the next morning, I went shopping for the 'promotion party'. I came back home and cooking started in earnest.

Daddy and kids came back from church service, the smell of my cooking must have been legendary; maybe the worship songs in the air further gingered their zeal as I received help here and there and especially with tasting of the food.

While dashing upstairs to take a shower and freshen up, I heard "Wasteful woman, foolish woman, is this the time to celebrate?" and to that I quickly retorted, "Shut up Satan, I'm not a stranger to your whims, this is promotion and we are coming out stronger. I'm still connected to heaven and can't afford to disappoint them now. I'm born of God and I overcome always" (I John 5:4).

Close to 6.00pm that evening, the bell started to ring announcing arrival of guests. By 7.15pm, the house was packed full. Whether the turnout was out of empathy, curiosity or to show respect, I cannot tell but the attendance was wow despite such short notice.

So, as much as we could, we gathered round the dining table to pray and I led praise with a Portuguese song:

Por tudo que tens feito (For all that You have done)
Por tudo que vai fazer (For all that You will do)
Por tuas promessas (For all Your promises)
E tudo que e, (And everything that is)
Eu quero te agradecer com todo meu ser (I want to appreciate You with all of my being)
Eu Te agradeço meu Senhor....... (I appreciate You, my Lord)

Then the dam broke, and many started to weep at that point. Even the men had misty eyes. Such expressions of sentiments!

But I felt God at that point. With mixed emotions, I realized I may not be seeing many of these people present again. I had come to love and closely relate with many since July 2008. But then I thought, definitely, He didn't bring us this far to dump us in the high sea. He's not a God of abandoned projects…. Surely God is in the midst of her, she shall not be moved and He would help right at the break of day.

²Therefore we will not fear,
Even though the earth be removed,
And though the mountains be carried into the midst of the sea;
³Though its waters roar and be troubled,
Though the mountains shake with its swelling. Selah
*⁵**God is in the midst of her, she shall not be moved;***
God shall help her, just at the break of dawn (Psalm 46:2,3,5).

And it occurred to me as we sang further that one had been a great benefactor of grace and guidance; per time the Lord shows up.

Hope and courage were fired back in my bones at this point as I held hands with the husband of my youth.

No shame Lord!

They looked to Him and were radiant, and their faces were not ashamed (Psalm 34:5).

All the paths of the Lord are mercy and truth,
To such as keep His covenant and His testimonies (Psalm 25:10).

And we know that all things work together for good to those who love God, to those who are the called according to His purpose (Romans 8:28).

Thereafter we sang in English, Spanish, Portuguese again and even our local dialect, Yoruba as we had these nationalities present. We gave thanks, cut the cake, listened to a few colleagues' comment on the celebrant and then it was time to dig into the food.

A Brazilian colleague of his at work commented saying, "I really do not understand this family, something very sad happened and you invited us for a party? You are strange people... I do wish you all the best in your future endeavours and don't forget: My family and I love you all and will always remember you".

With his hands in his pocket, my husband simply smiled. And standing next to him, I responded,

"A fe pode canta na tristeza, vai tudo bem" meaning: Surely faith can sing through days of sorrow for all will be well. You see, Jesus gives His own people strength."

Very strange we are, very different. A people unique, peculiar, set apart. A royal Priesthood must always show forth the praises of the heavenly Father.

But you are a chosen generation, a royal priesthood, a holy nation, His own special people, that you may proclaim the praises of Him who called you out of darkness into His marvelous light (1 Pet 2:9).

And the night ended on a glorious note with many lives impacted. Our joy was full. We all retired to bed exhausted but fulfilled.

The days which followed were trying.

The Monday right after, he had gone to the office to hand over his laptop and negotiate for our extended stay till the end of school year so the kids could complete their session. That period would also serve as an ample opportunity for us to seek God for direction.

Sincerely, his dismissal caught us unawares.

Prior to his dismissal from work, he had planned a trip to his home country Nigeria. We decided he should still progress with that, I also felt the change might do him some good and who knows? Opportunities might open. It was meant to be a 10 days trip anyway.

And travel he did.

While he was away, we sought God at both ends. A tough job seeking or hearing God when there's so much noise going on within you. However, the Psalmist in chapter 27 had declared the Lord as his light and the light of his life and of who or what should he fear.

With a consistent walk with the Lord prior to troubles coming, no need to be afraid. His leading and His victory will surely come.

My husband was due to return from Nigeria but at the airport, he discovered his visa had been cancelled by the company. We were stuck in Macae and he, stranded in Lagos.

After a month, the company decided to grant him access to the country but he was given just a stipulated period of stay.

During his period away, much of our planning was via telephone. Time was running out. We agreed to sell off some of our belongings while the other stuff would be shipped. The fact is that we were not sure where we were headed to. And as we sought Him for direction, we deliberated, strategized.

And then He showed up! The Holy Ghost. And His voice came through:

"You seem excited about the move. Where are you going? Have I told you it's over? Are you walking out of my plans for you now? I have an exam set for you here, you need to prepare, there is a set date for that. Or are you willing to repeat class? Or deferring at this point? Or dropping out of my plans for you?"

So, I woke from that encounter. While I felt relieved at hearing His voice, I had gradually gotten used to the idea that we were leaving. But for the eyes of faith, I was wondering how all would turn out. At least the end result was clear and sure now: The Lord still wanted us in Brazil.

And I will always remember that without His leading, one could repeat class in the school of glory without realizing it. Aligning closely to His will is the only way for promotion. Little wonder we must always acknowledge Him in all our ways for directions to come.

Trust in the Lord with all your heart,
And lean not on your own understanding;
⁶ In all your ways acknowledge Him,
And He shall direct your paths (Proverbs 3:5-6).

We, however, needed to trust without understanding how He the Master Strategist would work all out; but pressure was mounting and time was running out.

After that encounter, I stopped selling any more items. Already I had sold my husband's car and mine was already up for offer too. So, I refrained and resolved to keep mine in a friend's place pending the miracle of return to Brazil that the Lord had promised.

While in Nigeria, he had broken the news to our parents.

On an occasion, my mother called and asked if we had decided on where to relocate to.

I responded that we weren't sure yet.

"You people should come back home. Bring my grandchildren home. If they don't want you there, we want you here. In fact, we will all be at the airport to receive you back…a royal welcome it will be, I promise...."

Such were the kinds of words we received. I once had to reply a friend who stylishly chipped in that God gave us brains for many reasons but I had an answer ready for her.

"It is very true dear; our brains should function. It is also true that the blood of Jesus washed my sins away and not my brains but I still choose to wait for His leading. This brain must exercise restraint now. I know how He deals with me...... It is always better to move slowly behind Him rather than jumping ahead of His leading. In this scenario, a believer makes no haste". Isaiah 28:16 says,

Therefore thus says the Lord God:
"Behold, I lay in Zion a stone for a foundation,
A tried stone, a precious cornerstone, a sure foundation;
Whoever believes will not act hastily

And the company mounted pressure too in a bid to get us out of the accommodation and out of the country.

A man they had celebrated so much for generating outstanding revenue in his first year of arrival suddenly became a thorn in their flesh. The same set that chanted Hosanna at Christ's triumphant entry into Jerusalem also shouted, 'Crucify him'. But you see, it's all part of the plan. God is a Master Strategist.

They were asking for a date to come move our belongings and needed to know our destination. And to that, my husband replied that he would inform them.

Discomfort descended.

And then, one day, an email came from one company where he had applied for a job. They were asking if he could meet with the management for a discussion...... and the rest is history!

As we moved out of the house in Macae December 2010, we headed for a service apartment in Rio. Our belongings were all packed by the moving company. Still we weren't sure where exactly we were headed.

This faith walk sure makes one look stupid but at the end it always speaks! And God honours those who wait on Him most.

The former company had called asking where to ship our goods and all my husband said was, "I will let you know once I'm sure".

"Sir, we don't have all the time, storage costs money......."

Then the children asked me, "But why doesn't Daddy know?" They had overheard the telephone conversation.

"You see, children, we will do nothing except it be commanded from above, we just need to be sure of where God wants us to go and not just reason it out ourselves".

"All this while? You people still don't know?" My daughter asked.

"Well, sometimes God takes His time but you can be sure He will speak, Mommy is so sure God will speak. And He does so at the right time"

"Yeah, He is always telling you things", she muttered as she turned to continue playing games on their Nintendo Wii.

And then, an email came in for my husband. It was from the company he had been discussing with. An offer letter came through. The next day, it was a call from the HR of this new company.

Many things were discussed.

"...Sir, while we process your visa for return to Brazil. We kindly request you proceed to your home country. We would do everything to speed up your visa process......"

As I overheard that part of the conversation, I experienced a bout of emotions: I felt so proud of God proving true concerning our return to Brazil. But returning to Nigeria didn't go down so well. Why? I thought briefly about where we would stay. My parents place? At my in-laws? Visiting for a short stay was one thing and staying for months till visa was ready was another.

I let my swirling thoughts out to my husband and he reassured me we would be alright and that even if we had to stay at relations, it would all be short lived.

My voice must have carried some contrition as I saw sadness hang over him.

I resolved to behave myself wisely like David (1 Samuel 18), it was only temporary anyway. Is there any condition a missionary can't handle? I need not overburden this man with weightless matters.

But news from afar got better by the day.

Another call came through from this new company saying the Lagos office was expecting our arrival and that accommodation was being sorted in Lagos.

So, we informed the former company to ship our things to Lagos, Nigeria. We relocated January ending, 2011.

During our stay in Nigeria, our kids bonded with family and embraced some of the culture therein.

We stayed in Nigeria for precisely 3 months and ten days.

Shortly before the visa came through, the Lord made it clear: "Go and start my work fully".

The embassy had contacted us to pick our visas by third week in April. On that same day, we received a call from Brazil saying the inspection of our belongings was just completed after much delays and paper work and was set to sail for Lagos the next day.

"Hold my shipment right there, I'm on our way back. Shipping won't be necessary anymore" was the response my husband gave.

Who says God doesn't rule over the affairs of men? Even our

belongings were of interest to Him.

"So, first thing we need to do on arrival there is to get you a car.…...?" I asked him.

"Oh! Didn't you see in the offer documents? A company car is attached; your selling my car worked together for our good as well. And you still have yours so we are good. We praise God for all things".

And I marvelled at this God! He's involved in every affair of ours.

And just like Joseph within the same country, it was a move from prison to palace.

We announced to the children that it was time to go back.

"Really? Not Canada, not Aberdeen?"

"No, it's Brazil, you see, we must go back to where the Lord has in mind for us. If we go anywhere else, it will be disobedience and His blessings will not locate us. He has given Daddy another job there and has told us we must go and do His work fully now. Remember, we must serve Him anywhere He sends us".

"But Mommy, we prefer those two other places.…"

"Remember Lot in Genesis 13? He chose by sight. It is not about the benefits or convenience we would reap in a place but being sure His presence is with us. I repeat, we must be where He wants us to be. Didn't Father Abraham prosper in that same place that Lot thought was dry? Those places may be okay for others because God called them there but when you go on your own, you will struggle.

So, we returned and landed in Brazil May 2nd, 2011.

Re-energized and charged to raise a banner for my Lord and King in that land.

My Yoruba instinct reminded me of a proverb that says when a ram reverses or retreats initially it naturally returns with renewed strength and vigour.

The devil is a liar!

Who is he that saith, and it cometh to pass, when the Lord commandeth it not? (Lamentations 3:37, KJV).

The gates of Brazil had been lifted.

Lift up your heads, O ye gates; and be ye lift up, ye everlasting doors; and the King of glory shall come in (Psalm 24:7, KJV).

As we disembarked at Galeao International Airport in Rio De Janeiro that fateful evening of May 2nd and I stepped on the soil again I muttered under my breath:

"Blessed is she that cometh in the name of the Lord". Hallelujah!

Chapter 8

~

Baby Benjamin

THE YEAR 2015 HAD ME MAKING CERTAIN health changes about myself. Alongside documenting new visions for the year, there was just this urge within me to take charge of my body.

Not that there was any threat to my health. The urge to keep fit, and maintain a healthy lifestyle became uppermost. It was more like I suddenly jolted back into reality and hence, self-consciousness; it was just a reawakening period for me. I decided to add exercise to my weekly routine. Even the Holy Word adjoins that *bodily exercise profiteth little* (1Timothy 4vs8) hence I chose to profit from that 'little'. I however needed a medical certification to be sure I was fit for any physical activity.

An appointment was booked with a general practitioner to certify my medical fitness for physical activity. She had queried when I last did a full medical check-up.

Ever since the Lord miraculously healed me of ovarian cancer in 2009, I had never visited the hospital for any reason, not even for the annual checks which was a general rule. She generalized that it was strongly recommended for women over the age of 40 to observe annual check-up and strongly counselled I see a gynaecologist who would administer a thorough check-up, to which I willingly succumbed. The tests were all-embracing including blood works, cardio fitness, mammogram, swap tests and all tests imaginable at different labs. When all results were out, the lady gynaecologist invited me for a chat. She readjusted her glasses and asked how many children I had. I responded that I had two. In the same manner which I had been used to hearing medical practitioners give diagnosis, she looked at me seriously and said "it's a good thing you decided to do a full medical check-up at a time like this. And then in her Portuguese accent she explained that everything appears okay from results as she had taken time to analyse all. She noticed however that I had so many growths within the walls of my stomach and uterus and had asked if I experience any pains either in the past or presently to which I affirmed in the negative.

Further to her comments, she explained that it came to her as a relief that I had two children as chances of subsequent conception was less than 10%. At that news, my eyes dilated; she then explained that my uterus was lined with multiple fibroid and the sizes were quite enormous hence her asking if I regularly experienced any pain. She then gave a lecture on fibroid, until I got lost in my own thoughts. She must have gone on for about 7 – 10 minutes on this lecture. The conclusion of the matter was that I was to be closely monitored from time to time till time was ripe for surgery. For once, I wondered how David must have felt when he had to face Goliath. If only the Philistines knew he had wrestled and killed a bear and a lion before in the wilderness, their ranting and boastful words would have been minimized. My faith had been built to believe God for greater things, petty matters like fibroid wouldn't move me. Neither did I give any surgery a thought.

The next scheduled visit was to be in six weeks' time. That would be for exams to further confirm the fibroids growth rate lining my uterus. I was given some prescription that day. As I stepped out of the hospital that fateful evening, I looked up to heaven and said, "Father, thank you, multiple fibroid is too small for you to clear…" and just as I was rounding up my prayer, my immediate younger sister called. We chatted and I explained I was just leaving the hospital premises where a gynaecologist had just diagnosed multiple fibroid and that worst part was when she mentioned my chances of conceiving was less than 10%. That really got me angry in my spirit and if for anything, I wanted to prove her wrong. Sincerely, I desired another baby for once after 12 years of my last conception. My sister jokingly mentioned that I should have told the doctor that I serve a God who supplied me with miracles per time. She said having another baby would be nice and that she would be willing to adopt the baby from me. I had chided her that she would have hers and not adopt mine. We then laughed and discussed other issues.

Life continued as usual with physical exercise now becoming a regular routine. Daily, my stamina increased and I was becoming physically fit. I started receiving compliments on how fit and youthful I had become and that only motivated me further to keep at it. In no distant time, I opted for the staircase instead of the elevator as we lived in an 8-floor apartment. I felt like I was fully in-charge of my body. A new wave of strength was evident; my thinking became clearer. I would sleep for a few hours and wake up feeling refreshed. Even my self-confidence received a boost. Having the best time of my life was an understatement in expressing how I felt.

And then, in the morning of Saturday the 1st of May 2015, my son and I had returned home from his basketball practice and as was now my custom, I had decided to use the stairs instead of the elevator. On reaching the floor of my apartment, I suddenly experienced this fainting spell. I felt I must have overworked my body in the past week, I also recollected I had earlier done some brisk walking while my son was at practice that morning and thought that would have been the cause of the feeling.

That same day, as we packed my husband's bags for a business trip, I had this funny feeling again.

And then, during the following week I experienced the same feeling twice. On the third occasion, I couldn't make it to the 8th floor but had to stop midway and take the elevator up. Thoughts of what could be wrong bugged my mind and I decided to mention this to the gynaecologist on my next appointment which was less than ten days away. It then occurred to me that I hadn't taken the medications she gave, as a matter of fact, they were all forgotten in the handbag I used during that visit to the hospital in March!

I couldn't wait to confirm what was happening to me. Recollecting vividly, fainting spells were synonymous to pregnancy for me;

possibilities? Can it be? Much later that evening, I stopped by at a pharmacy to get a pregnancy test kit. The advice was to test my urine early the next morning for best result. It took forever for 6.00am the next day to arrive as I checked the time intermittently. It must have felt like eternity for the test kit to show the result. Lo and behold, It turned pink; I was pregnant! Sincerely, my feelings were mixed, I felt my whole life crashing right before me as I had my plans all laid out before me without anything unplanned intruding. I burst out subconsciously, 'Ha! 9 months imprisonment, 4 years hard labour!!'. Immediately, I repented and asked for forgiveness realizing I had close friends that I was also trusting God to grant the fruit of the womb. Again, I was elated at the thought of that doctor being proved wrong— either God overheard my conversation with my sister that fateful day in March as I left the hospital after receiving the news of a 10% chance of conception due to fibroid, or He just chose to honour my faith by my refusing the womb from being evacuated during the ovarian cancer ordeal so a baby Benjamin could actually come forth. Or perhaps, He had predestined another fruit of the womb as a reward. Either way, let the name of the Lord be magnified.

As I laid in bed afterwards, I tried recollecting dates of my last menstrual period in a bid to calculate how advanced the pregnancy was. Unfortunately, keeping such records wasn't my strength especially since my last pregnancy was well over 12 years ago. As I ruminated, two dreams I had in April the previous month flashed through my mind.

In the first dream, I had dozed off on a sofa and suddenly found myself lactating. On waking up, I wondered why I would lactate in my dream. As I meditated on that, I dozed off again and this time around, I saw myself lactating profusely with my blouse fully drenched. I had concluded then that lactating had to do with nurturing but what was I to nurture precisely? Disciples?

At that point, it all made sense, the Holy Spirit had tried to hint me about the pregnancy!!

Well, the appointment day came and as I sat before the gynaecologist, she was just particular about knowing if I was experiencing any pain, I told her I had news for her. As I informed her that I was pregnant, she told me it was not possible based on her analysis from the lab result. I affirmed that I was and that I had done a urine test. Quite unprofessional of her but she insisted it was not possible and that she would recommend I get a proper pregnancy test done and that if it was ever positive, I needed to stop taking the drugs she last prescribed and that I would require very close monitoring due to the fibroid growth. As she spoke, the dreams flashed again and I just smiled being fully reassured that all was well. As a matter of fact, the Holy Spirit revealed the sex of the baby that same period.

So, the lab result confirmed the pregnancy was in its 7th week. I must have conceived shortly after that first meeting with the gynaecologist, that very month of March in which she gave me the fibroid report and a 90% certainty of no possible conception. My husband and our two kids were shocked at the pregnancy news. However, we praised God for all things. We became eager to meet this 'son of our old age' as father Jacob described Benjamin in the scriptures. The period of pregnancy sure had its normal challenge as it had been a wee while. The experience at well over 40 years of age was nothing compared to that of late 20s'. As much as I could, I enjoyed the pregnancy phase, rejoicing in the Lord every month, flaunting my protruding tommy and even taking regular photo shoots in appreciation of what the Lord was doing in my life. God was faithful all through the nine months. Our baby Benjamin was born a few minutes to 9.00am on the 20th of December 2015 at the maternity hospital called Perinatal Laranjeiras, Rio De Janeiro. Inception of labour till delivery was all within 3 hours. Despite all reports, God defied every medical explanation to show His Sovereignty and precisely nine months after that report from the gynaecologist.

Precisely six weeks after delivery, I had visited my gynaecologist with my baby for a post natal check up. She confirmed all was well with me, the varied fibroids were all shrunk and never became an issue anymore. The doctor further advised annual check ups and that any pain should be reported for a check up.

As I pen this down, it is over two years and no traces of any pain. The Egyptian I saw, I see them no more! Those multiple growing cells must have all served as pillows for our baby while in the womb.

Ascribing glory to God is the thin line that marks a difference between boasting and making a boast in God.

Shall we exalt His name together?

Chapter 9

∽

Charge to the Believer

F AITH COMES BY HEARING AND HEARING by the word of God (Romans 10:17). The expectation of God is that a believer diligently feeds on His word and then acts on those words.

James 1v25b says: *"but a doer of the word, this man shall be **blessed in his deed**"* (KJV).

It is in the 'doing' that the blessings are received.

We must not just hear and forget lest we become like the man described by Apostle James, who after looking in the mirror leaves and forgets what he looks like (James 1:23-24).

For if anyone is a hearer of the word and not a doer, he is like a man observing his natural face in a mirror; [24] ***for he observes himself, goes away, and immediately forgets what kind of man he was*** *(NKJV).*

As we hear and receive understanding, we are better equipped to act in line with the words we have received. If I do not have faith, it is not God's fault. Blaming Him for lack of faith reveals ignorance as God has made every provision available. Growing my faith is solely my responsibility and I can't hold anyone else accountable for that. I alone can make my faith grow. The kind of faith that can turn weakness to strength.

Feed your spirit through diligent study of the word, reading faith-building books and listening to spirit-filled messages. It all comes by the hearing and permit me to add, 'by the reading'.

What you hear and read have a way of registering into your spirit. You feed your faith with the word of God and that represents the seed and as you continually hear the word again and again, you water the seed further with the word and faith building commences. Feed not your spirit on what the news or friends have to offer. With faith building through the word, faith and truth come and so does triumph over every storm of life. Though there's intent to share more on faith boosters in another booklet titled **Faith Nuggets,** permit me at this point to share three practical tips to an ever-growing faith.

One sure avenue of building faith is fellowshipping with other believers such that you are exposed to 'hearing faith-building words'. Every believer right from the day of accepting the Lord is enjoined to fellowship with the family of God. Hebrews 10v25,

*...**not forsaking the assembling of ourselves together,** as is the manner of some, but exhorting one another, and so much the more as you see the Day approaching.*

Little wonder we are admonished in the book of Hebrews to never forsake the gathering of other believers. Truly, we become the company we keep and so association with people of like minds is required. God is in the fellowship of the saints.

*For where two or three are gathered together in My name, **I am there in the midst of them*** (Matthew 18v20).

It is not about who is leading such meetings but God who assured us of His presence there. The fellowship of saints is referred to as Zion.

*But you have come to **Mount Zion and to the city of the living God, the heavenly Jerusalem, to an innumerable company of angels,** [23] **to the general assembly and church of the firstborn who are registered in heaven,** to God the Judge of all, to the spirits of just men made perfect, [24] to Jesus the Mediator of the new covenant, and to the blood of sprinkling that speaks better things than that of Abel* (Hebrews 12v22-24, NKJV).

Our lives are serviced at Zion and that is why we refer to church meeting attendance as 'service'.

The enemy will do anything to keep us away from fellowship and once we are out of fellowship for some time, our defence is down. Fellowship is a mystery for staying in faith. Divine presence is guaranteed at fellowship and faith levels are changed thereby.

An illustration a teacher of the word cited is the example of firewood when gathered together. The wood all glow being ignited by one another. However, there is a high tendency that when one plank is taken away from the bunch for a while, it begins to lose the fire and eventually fizzle out. A wood that was initially hot on fire can then became a host for insects and anything else to perch upon.

Faith goes down when we are out of fellowship with God's people.

It is best left to imagination what a once vibrant believer can do when out of fellowship for a short while. An illustration given by a father figure in the faith on the importance of fellowship for any believer explained that no matter how strong a lion is, it can never face a rhino alone. It takes a group of lions to conquer a rhino!

Ever sat amid people who complain and discuss negative reports on any situation? You leave such company low in your spirit and hopeless and vice versa if you are in the right company.

Saul was only able to prophesy because he was in the company of prophets. Faith is bound to rise during fellowship with brethren; and with fellowship comes strength.

Christ Jesus our Lord was always in fellowship and as a matter of fact one of the first things he did while launching into ministry was to quickly organize fellowship around Himself (Mark 3v14).

*Then **He appointed twelve, that they might be with Him** and that He might send them out to preach.*

We must never toy with fellowship as it is one thing that keeps a believer going Ecclesiastes 4v10.

For if they fall, one will lift up his companion.
But woe to him who is alone when he falls,
For he has no one to help him up.

According to Hebrews 12v23-24, we renew our citizenry at every fellowship,

...to the general assembly and church of the firstborn who are registered in heaven, to God the Judge of all, to the spirits of just men made perfect, [24] to Jesus the Mediator of the new covenant, and to the blood of sprinkling that speaks better things than that of Abel (NKJV).

Secondly, listening to testimonies surely builds faith. The essence of sharing and hearing testimonies is for faith to increase. What God did for one, He can yet do for another and even much more as we anchor on to faith in our hearts. God has never changed through the ages and His principles of acting in the affairs of men remains ever constant. He said in Malachi that He is God and He does not change.

"For I am the Lord, I do not change; Therefore you are not consumed, O sons of Jacob (Malachi 3v6, NKJV).

Every testimony is prophetic. Truly the testimony of Jesus is the spirit of prophecy. Anywhere testimonies are being shared, God is in that vicinity to see as many hearts as can trust Him to move in their circumstances. They are highly powered "arrows" ordained to deliver and reproduce in the lives of as many as will key into such testimonies.

Your testimonies I have taken as a heritage forever, For they are the rejoicing of my heart (Psalm 119v111, NKJV).

Many have received their own breakthroughs by keying into the testimony of others.

Testimony remains a powerful weapon for overcomers; as a matter of fact, it is grouped in the same class as the blood of Jesus which is the ultimate and most powerful weapon in defeating the enemy.

*And they overcame him by the blood of the Lamb **and by the word of their testimony**, and they did not love their lives to the death* (Revelation 12v11, NKJV).

David had clearly used this weapon to bring Goliath down.

[34] *But David said to Saul, "Your servant used to keep his father's sheep, and when a lion or a bear came and took a lamb out of the flock,* [37] *Moreover David said, "**The Lord, who delivered me from the paw of the lion and from the paw of the bear, He will deliver me from the hand of this Philistine.**" And Saul said to David, "Go, and the Lord be with you!"* (1 Sam 17v34, 37, NKJV).

I therefore submit that testimonies remain a hidden source of faith building. Testimonies carry power, power of reaffirmation. Testimonies are ordained to empower one for next victories. Past testimonies, when declared, provoke future victories. The devil cannot play down testimonies; they are effective arrows in the day of battle. The power of testimony is everlasting. Psalm 119:144 says,

The righteousness of Your testimonies is everlasting;
Give me understanding, and I shall live (NKJV).

Thirdly, giving attention to the word. Proverbs 4v2 says: "My son, pay attention to my word, incline thine ears to my saying". In paying attention, you consciously become a student of the word. The word must find meanings and expression in you. An illustration I've come to appreciate in relating with this, is the process by which food is absorbed into our bodies.

Food eaten has no benefit until it is digested and broken down to the various food classes like carbohydrate, proteins, fats and oil. These are then transported into the blood for effective use. In the same vein, the word of God may have no effect even though quoted except it is meditated upon and ruminated over. The word must leave the head and finding its way into the heart of man. Faith cometh by hearing, hearing by the word of God. (Romans 10:17).

A story was once told of a woman who had worked very closely and faithfully with a queen in a certain country. They became so intimate such that the queen virtually entrusted everything to her. At the queen's demise, this worker was given a small certificate while the queen's inheritance was shared by her relatives. The faithful worker hung this little certificate on the wall in her home and proudly showed everyone who visited her; for this she was always applauded. She took ill after a while and it got worse by the day. At a point, she couldn't afford to pay for medicals bills anymore. While a doctor visited with her on her sick bed, she referred to the certificate. The doctor out of curiosity decided to take a closer look at the small certificate. Lo, and behold! In small but bold prints, it read that the queen had willed all she had to this faithful woman! She was dying of ill health due to abject poverty while the key to prosperity hung on her wall. Beloved, we can lack knowledge of what God has provided if we don't study the Word.

Faith will not come if we do not study. While I grew in the faith, I found out that often my mind gets distracted while studying so I often have to read the word out loud to my very own hearing. I must hear, hearing by the word! Acts 20:32 says, "*So now, brethren, I commend you to God and to **the word of His grace, which is able to build you up** and give you an inheritance among all those who are sanctified*" (NKJV).

The impact of the word is best related to a sponge that is soaked in water, you never know how drenched the sponge is until pressure is applied on it by squeezing. When life throws challenges at us, what should ooze out must be the water of the word that we have consciously given a place in our hearts. Faith grows with the word level in us, as a matter of fact, there is an assurance that comes by the knowing of the word. Just like you cannot use the fuel in my car to drive your car, in the same vein you cannot study for me to pass an exam. It is impossible that I can be built up as an individual except I give myself wholly to building personally by the word. As more light comes from the word, the God-kind of confidence is increased which is the faith needed to access more of my inheritance in Christ. You see, when you are convinced on any matter based on your discovery from scripture, no devil can confuse you.

There is no report I can receive from a medical practitioner that can move me now. Why? I have received light in that aspect of my life. I may not react immediately in the presence of the practitioner but I know that He that is above, is above all. The doctor and I may not operate on the same frequency. I know that Jesus already bore my sicknesses, scripture says He was wounded for my transgression and by His stripes **I have been made whole** (Isaiah 53v5).

Having been through the ordeals of appendicitis, ovarian cancer, and multiple fibroid yet divinely healed of all, I trust that no matter what comes my way, 2 Corinthians 1 verse 10 stands sure:

...who delivered us from so great a death, and does deliver us; in whom we trust that He will still deliver us (NKJV).

Ever wondered why David was so bold before Goliath? He ignored fear by not considering the size of Goliath but the size of his God. He was fully persuaded that the same God who delivered the lion and the bear into his hands would do the same of Goliath. What has God given you victory over in the past? Build on that—He is able and willing to do much more if you let Him. Though faith can be categorized into compartments, the same faith that is required for healing is the same faith required for biological conception, financial breakthroughs, deliverances, as well as for raising the dead.

Friends, all things are yours if you believe.

The Ultimate Call

DEAR READER, I BELIEVE YOU HAVE been blessed with faith being fired up on the inside. God is ever waiting to show Himself strong on our behalf as we stay focused on Him. Much as I rejoice in His various dealings in my life and the way He constantly granted me victory, I celebrate more the fact that my name has been written in the book of life (Luke 10:20).

It is the greatest miracle and a man's salvation is his greatest testimony.

So, I will like to ask you this very important question:

"Is your name written in the book of life?"

Without this, it is a straight route to hell (Revelation 20 v15).

There is an urgent need to decide for Jesus and borrowing the words of Billy Graham, "a decision you delay in making will decide against you eventually as time really waits for no one."

Only you have the power to decide where you will be a hundred years from now. You may have tried all and still lack the power to live for Him. Paraphrasing John 1:11v13, "To as many as received Him gave He power to be called the sons of God. Even to as many as call on His name".

The true Christian walk is only made possible by the power in that name Jesus as He is willing to fill you with the Holy Spirit who will enable you run the Christian race well to the very end. All you need is repentance – being willing to turn from your old ways and acknowledge your need of Him.

To accept Him, please repeat this prayer below:

Lord Jesus, I thank you. I acknowledge I have tried to run my life on my own. I confess I am a sinner in need of you. Please cleanse me by your blood, I invite you in as Lord and Saviour of my life. Please fill my heart and give me the grace to walk with you to the end. Thank you for hearing me, in Jesus name I pray. AMEN.

If you have truly said this prayer from your heart, I congratulate and welcome you into the family of God. Surely the heavens rejoice over you and your name is written in the Lamb's book of life.

Trust the Lord to lead you to a true Bible-believing church, where you can identify with real fellowship for growth and true discipleship. I pray that the Lord uphold you to the end. Amen.

Is God still in the business of honouring faith in His word today? This write up is a resounding affirmation to the fact that active faith still produces results in a hopeless world as we have today.

Temi Fagade, an ardent believer in the word of faith teaching, shares in this book her true life experiences of God's gracious dealings with her as she trusted Him for diverse victories and varied triumphs in life's storms. Her anchor has remained faith in God's words.

Not A Stranger To Storms is an inspirational piece revealing testimonies of God's faithfulness in aspect of healings, overcoming trials of parenting, conception amongst other challenging situations. Absolute trust in God for all whims in life's sojourn are represented herein and as such, makes this book of testimonies **a must read** for all and sundry.

Temi is an ordained minister of the gospel with a heart for missions. She received a call in an early morning vision on the 29th of July 2006 in Aberdeen, Scotland with the mandate to go give hope to the hopeless, strengthen feeble knees and to give direction to lives.

Being passionately involved in varied mission efforts in Brazil led to planting and pioneering *The Church of All Nations* in Macae, Rio de Janeiro together with her husband. She is a mother of three covenant children. She is an intercessor, writer and researcher.

Please contact Temi via her email address,
temifagade@gmail.com

www.ingramcontent.com/pod-product-compliance
Lightning Source LLC
Chambersburg PA
CBHW071538040426
42452CB00008B/1060